Nine Thousand Miles to Adventure

A Story of an American Boy in the Philippines

John P. Santacroce

Four Oaks Publishing

Copyright © 2018 John P. Santacroce

All rights reserved.

ISBN: 0989991601
ISBN-13: 978-0989991605

For my children
Zachary, Christopher and Matthew

CONTENTS

CHAPTER 1 1
- Biloxi, Mississippi 1972 1
- Geography Lesson 2
- The Map 4
- First Impressions 4
- Driving Home 6
- Fortress House 8
- Lizards and Pigs 8
- Water 9
- Spider Fights 10
- Sari-Sari 11
- Our New Life 11

CHAPTER 2 13
- First Day of School 13
- The School Bus 14
- Bullets on the Ground 14
- The Legend of Lily Hill 16
- EOD 18
- Elephant Grass 19
- Snakes 21
- Charlie the Snake 24
- The Perimeter 25
- "Robbed!" 27
- "Mayday! Mayday!" 28
- Falling Trees 29
- Layover in Saigon 30
- The Crossbow 32

CHAPTER 3 33
- A Boring Saturday 33
- Trading at the Perimeter 35
- The Trap 36

Warnings	37
The Chase	38
The Holes	39
Help	40
The Dogs	43
The Hero	45

CHAPTER 4 47

Boy Scouts	47
Jungle Summer Camp	48
Rain	49
Parachute Hammocks	50
Rats	50
Muck Field	51
Jungle Campsite	52
Mosquito Nets	52
Rifling Merit Badge	53
The Marine	54
Moving Target	56
Tents in the Jungle	56
Mudfish	57
Fruit Bats	58
Wild Monkeys	59
First Sighting	60
The Snare	61
Monkey Escape	63

CHAPTER 5 65

Crow Valley	65
City in the Sky	65
Camp O'Donnell	66
Beagles and Pirates	67
Scoutmasters	67
Dad the Scout Leader	69
Ant Attack	69
Coconuts	70
The Bamboo Table and RED HORSE	70
Jungle Survival Training: Day One	72

- Jungle Survival Training: Day Two 74
- Nightfall 75
- Jungle Survival Training: Day Three 76
- The Hunter 76

CHAPTER 6 78
- The Greatest Camping Trip 78
- Capture the Flag 79
- The Discovery 80
- The Bomb 80
- The Plan 81
- Airplane Graveyard Raid 82
- RB-66 84
- Captured 85
- Back to the Bomb 86
- The Flare 87
- Counter-attack 88
- Dad and the Bomb 89
- Floor Towels 91
- Clobbering Time 92

CHAPTER 7 94
- The Library 94
- Bataan 95
- Death March 96
- Fifty Miler 97
- Rabbit Buses 98
- Memorials 99
- Fifty Miles in Three Days 99
- The Joke 100
- Camping on the Beach 101
- The Bonfire 102
- Jungle Fever 103
- Saved by a Rabbit Bus 105
- Corregidor 106
- Bonka Boats 107

CHAPTER 8 110

    Corregidor Revisited 110
    The Forty Millimeter 111
    The Missing Mortar 112
    The Last Adventure 114
    Tunnels 114
    Another Plan 115
    Unimaginable Treasure 115
    Damage Control 117
    Back Inside 118
    Lost Secrets 119
    The Mysterious Man 120
CHAPTER 9 122
    Treasures: Found and Lost 122
    The Home Run 122
    Incident at Friendship Gate 123
    Wars: Past and Present 123
    The Searchers 124
    LINEBACKER 124
    Prisoners of War 125
    Babylift 125
    The Filipino Spirit 125
    My Bike 126
    The Amnesty Box and Charlie 127
    Travis Air Force Base, California 1975 127
CHAPTER 10 128
    Mount Pinatubo 128
    The Dictionary 129
    Memories 130
    Old Letters 131
ONE LAST THING 137
    The Philippine Frog Monster 137
A Note from the Author 146

FOREWARD

Why do people feel compelled to write books? I've asked myself that question for a long time. I'm happy to say I've finally found an answer. Well, at least my answer anyway. For several years I've been telling people about my childhood adventures in the Philippines. People seem to enjoy these stories immensely – often asking me to repeat them over and over. I have to admit the stories do seem to get better with time.

In January 1993 I brought my family to California. I was a Captain in the United States Air Force assigned to Los Angeles Air Force Base. We lived on Fort MacArthur, a beautiful little military housing reservation located in San Pedro overlooking the Los Angeles harbor. It was there I discovered the true and precious value of my youth.

One hot, sunny day I took my two sons, Zachary (5) and Christopher (2), on our own little adventure as we climbed and hiked all over an old coastal artillery site named Battery Osgood-Farley. The battery is located at the Fort MacArthur Upper Reservation overlooking the Santa Cruz Channel and Catalina Island. There was a time when the disappearing cannon of located there could hurl a several hundred-pound shell over 20 miles with devastating accuracy. But that was long ago. The artillery pieces are gone now. All that remain are the gun mounts and a small museum.

Everywhere I looked brought memories flooding back from my time in the Philippines: the concrete gun emplacements, the green and brown of the landscape, the sun beating down on my neck…and those smells! Especially the one smell – the one you can almost taste. It's a combination of searing heat, dusty roads, and dried brown grasses, occasionally intermingled with the musty dampness of the huge cement bunkers. It reminded me of the massive gun batteries of Corregidor, the island fortress located in the Bay of Manila. It brought back memories of the long, dusty road out of Bataan and of the immense lush plain of Clark Air Force Base.

As I sat there looking out over the channel, my son Zachary walked up to me. With a simple, "Look what I found, Dad!" I had my answer. There in his hand was an old, green-stained, spent cartridge casing, probably from a .30 caliber machine gun. Years ago some soldier must have fired from this very spot, either for practice or out of boredom. But now a small grinning boy held onto the shell. Forever a new memory linking the adventure of this day with those of his father's so many years past.

The simple pleasure of the moment was the key – being together, experiencing something new, re-living a memory from the past, being a part of something to remember forever. And for those reasons, I write this book. Lest I forget, the greatest thing in life is living. This book is about my adventures in the Philippines, 1972-1975. I'm writing it for my children. And their children. I'd like to thank everyone who made those years in the Philippines some of the best of my life. Especially my Mom and Dad.

John P. Santacroce – 1994

I awoke the next morning almost exactly in the same position I fell asleep in – crooked. I slowly began to regain my senses. Somewhat alarmed at first, I was surprised to find myself in a tree. It took me a few seconds to remember why…

Nine Thousand Miles to Adventure

CHAPTER 1

Biloxi, Mississippi 1972

My father was a Major in the United States Air Force stationed at Keesler Air Force Base, Mississippi. Stationed with him was his wife (my mom) and their eight children (my brothers and sisters.) My name is John and I was 11 years old. I was the fifth child born, and as such I was commonly referred to as "one of the four little kids," although not usually by my two older brothers. In fact, they very rarely even called me John. For some strange reason they called me "Jan Pan."

We lived in a red brick, four-bedroom house on Vandenberg Drive, a stone's throw from the Back Bay of Biloxi. I shared a room with my three brothers and two sets of bunk beds. My sisters always got the better deal – only two to a room.

Our time in Mississippi was drawing to a close. My father had received orders to the Philippines. The rumor was he originally received orders to Vietnam. When "they" found out Dad had eight dependent children, it was decided the Philippines was about as far West in the Far East as he needed to go. I guess the government didn't want to support my mom and eight children lest anything should happen to my dad.

Now we had moved before, but this time was different. I was clearly reaching the age of remembering. I had just entered the sixth grade at Jefferson Elementary school, a place where I started the third grade. No doubt about it, I was going to miss Biloxi.

It was there I first learned to fish. I recall the days spent crabbing on the Back Bay and the excitement of pulling in my six-foot casting net, heavy with fish from the Gulf of Mexico. Actually, my net would have been heavy if I happened to catch just one fish.

Once, some of us rode the ferry out to Ship Island with my dad. We used a t-shirt to seine for shrimp that day, and we actually caught a few! I even survived being a hit by a car while riding my bicycle to school. The lady who hit me screamed harder and longer than I did. I had my first real friendships in Biloxi, including my first girlfriend and first real kiss.

As a member of the neighborhood Rat Patrol, a harmless club based on the popular television show, I had my first real brush with the law. Of course, that's another story. I'll never forget hanging out on the base golf course, catching chameleons and turtles, trying to dig tunnels, and retrieving golf balls from the pond. The highlight, however, was when I saw a T-28 propeller airplane crash into Keesler Air Force Base's flight line. Yeah, I was going to miss Biloxi. I made grand plans to stay in touch with all my friends, but that never happened. I often wonder how they're doing.

I did make it back to Biloxi nineteen years later, though just for a day. It was hard to believe we all lived in that house!

Geography Lesson

My dad sat me and the other little kids down one day to explain just exactly where it was we were going. He took out the atlas and showed us where the Philippines was in relation to Biloxi. Cool, I thought, the Philippines were a bunch of islands. That's about all I remembered from the geography lesson.

I don't think I had any concept about just how far away it was and I didn't seem to care either. It wasn't such a big deal. The whole family was going. Everybody except Tony, the oldest kid in the family.

Tony is my oldest big brother. He graduated valedictorian from high school at 16 years of age and had a full scholarship to attend a private college near Chicago. He was, to say the least, very smart, and he was also an Eagle Scout. I remember he had all this cool stuff that I was always getting into: models, microscopes, a coin collection, and hundreds of little boxes full of thousands of neat things like wishbones, German money, and walnuts. He was the greatest pack rat I knew. I felt sorry for Tony because he always had to share a room with three little brothers, especially me. Even though Tony didn't travel to the Philippines with us initially, he did come to visit once. Even under those circumstances, I never forgot about him. He was the reason why I wanted to be a Boy Scout and why today I'm the biggest pack rat I know.

Dad had to travel to the Philippines without us for about six weeks to find us a place to live. The Vietnam War was still going on at the time. Outside of Vietnam and Thailand, the Philippines was home to one of the largest U. S. military installations in the world: Clark Air Force Base. It was the home of the 13th Air Force, which served as a major military communications hub for military forces in the Pacific and it had a busy flight line.

Housing on base was scarce, so Dad put us on the waiting list and found us a place to live off base. Before he left he told me I was responsible for helping mom while he was away. Specifically, he wanted me to make sure all his tools got to the Philippines; I think he was worried some would get lost or left behind. What an awesome responsibility, I thought. I recall poking my head in the shed once and a while to check up on things, but besides that, I don't think I did anything else. Although I missed my dad, I enjoyed the freedom from adult supervision; after all, Mom couldn't watch all of us. I think she may have even appreciated me for staying as far away from the house as possible.

The only problem with getting ready to leave was…the shots. The dreaded shots. I hated needles. We all had to be immunized for some unknown reason. I remember getting those shots before we left for Germany. Of course that was almost six years earlier, but I imagined I could still feel the pain in my arm. It was (and still is) a lingering, stabbing pain (ouch!).

I heard the words cholera and typhoid a lot. I remember the cholera shot especially well; it would temporarily paralyze the whole side of my body. Sort of like a dentist's shot numbing your mouth, except now half your body was useless for a day. I could feel the pain long before we got to the hospital.

Out of the whole family, I was the worst shot taker. Like a pack of animals that feeds on its wounded, my brothers and sisters milked the situation for all it was worth. I was teased without mercy. Miraculously, I survived.

The Map

Well, Dad found us a place and sent us a pretty detailed floor plan of the house. My first impression was that this was no ordinary house; it appeared to be a fortress. It was surrounded by a wall...a six-foot high wall. The only way in was through what looked like a big gate at the entrance to the driveway.

I can't forget showing the map to my friends, bragging that I was going to be living in a fort. It wasn't until later when I overheard my older brother and sister asking my mom why we were living in a house with a wall around it, that I began to wonder. Shortly after that is when I first heard the term "martial law." Apparently the Philippines was in the midst of a civil war. Minor problem, I thought. Small price to pay to live in a fort. It couldn't be any worse than being immunized. More than anything else, Dad's map made me want to go.

First Impressions

I don't remember the day we actually left Biloxi, just landing in Alaska. Our plane was stopping in Alaska? I looked at a map thinking this is nowhere near the Philippines. It's not even on the way. We must be on the wrong plane. I really got worried when I overheard our next destination was Japan. We were lost.

Mom assured me we were not lost. The world is round, she

explained, and maps are flat. She said the shortest route is not always the most obvious. Evidently Mom had too many kids to deal with and just couldn't comprehend the seriousness of the situation. Sure enough though, our plane made it to the Philippines. We landed without incident at Clark Air Force Base sometime in August 1972.

When I stepped out of the plane and walked down onto the tarmac, I saw a man casually standing off to the side from where we were departing. I was startled to see him holding an enormous knife in his hand. Instinctively, I moved closer to my dad. Slowly and carefully I whispered that a man with a towel wrapped around his head was holding a huge knife…and he was standing only about 20 feet away!

As if I were a distraction, Dad glanced down just long enough to say it was okay. How strange, I thought, that Dad wasn't even concerned. The man and I looked at each other for a while, then he turned and walked away. I noticed several men up and down portions of the runway near the terminal, all dressed similarly and holding a bolo (that's what you call a big knife in the Philippines…another name for a bolo is a machete). The men were bending over as they walked, swinging their bolos from side-to-side. They were cutting the grass! I had just seen my first Filipinos. They dressed so cool and they get to carry big knives around. Within a moment's time I had experienced fear, excitement, and intrigue. I had only just landed and already my adventure had begun.

As we walked to the terminal it seemed the sky was bigger than it had been in Biloxi. It was beautiful. Even the air seemed different. Looking out across the flight line, I could see green everywhere. It was almost as if we had landed in a huge tropical garden. Dominating the horizon lay Mount Arayat, a huge, dormant volcano jutting out of the plain to the East. It reminded me of Africa's great Mount Kilimanjaro.

Things were different inside the terminal. We weren't allowed to go near our luggage, although I could see it along with everybody else's in one giant pile. An American dressed in green fatigues shouldering a rifle and wearing a beret was letting his German shepherd dog walk all over the luggage. Dad said the dog was sniffing for firearms and drugs. Mark, one of my older brothers, said they were looking for dirty underwear. He said after they finished with the luggage pile the dog was going to come over and sniff us. I actually remember being a little worried.

We were all herded into a large briefing room where some soldier guy got up and welcomed us to the Philippines. He explained this and that, mentioned something about martial law, and generally went blah blah blah. My mind was elsewhere.

It sure was strange to see so many different looking people all at once. Off in side conversations, I could hear people talking, but I could not understand their words. They were speaking in Tagalog, the language of the Philippines. I saw one guy sweeping the floor with what looked like a two-foot-long bundle of sticks. In the Philippines, even the brooms were different.

Driving Home

After our initial in-processing, we all loaded up in an old, beat-up white station wagon. My dad had bought the car from some departing American family on their way back to the States. Very few people brought their own vehicles over with them. Shipping a car usually exceeded the maximum weight limit allowed per family. Once that happened it became an out-of-pocket expense which almost nobody could afford. Since it was next to impossible to find a new car to buy in the Philippines, once one did arrive on the islands it never left. Cars came here to die.

Cars were destined to be sold from person-to-person until they became totally unusable, which was rare. Despite the lack of auto parts, Filipino ingenuity could somehow keep them running forever. Come to think of it, I don't ever remember seeing any broken-down cars anywhere. There must've been a secret automobile graveyard hidden away somewhere in the jungle.

As we drove away from the airport I was amazed at how beautiful and different everything was. I was equally amazed at the number of aircraft I could see, especially military aircraft. There were cargo planes, bombers, and helicopters all up and down the flight line. It was a far cry from the little propeller-driven T-28s in Biloxi. What really caught my eye were the fighters. McDonnell Douglas F-4 Phantoms: big, powerful and lethal looking and almost all of them painted in the typical camouflage pattern of that era. And man, were they loud! As they streaked across the sky the noise from their engines would shake the ground. It was like watching thunder. To me it was just one more plus for living here. At the time I had no idea it was not all that uncommon for some of those planes to take off and never come back.

Dad drove us by the hospital (where he worked as a nurse), the commissary (where we could buy our food), the golf course, some of the schools (Clark Air Force Base had five schools) and on past the flight line. Eventually we reached the Friendship Gate.

On the other side of Friendship Gate lay Angeles City, a Filipino city just outside of the base. Clark Air Force Base was almost like a small rural American town. On the base side of Friendship Gate, the fields were immense and uncluttered. The roads were paved. Houses and buildings looked a lot like they did back in Mississippi. However, once you exited the gate you really knew you were no longer in the States. It was terribly crowded. Houses and other buildings, nothing more than shacks really, were crammed together along narrow, mostly unpaved roads. The place was bustling with activity. There were street vendors hocking all kinds of wood carvings and paintings as people strolled by. Strange smells filled the air. Mostly food smells, like that of the lumpia, a Filipino version of the eggroll. It wasn't long before lumpia and fried rice became household favorites. But a lot of those new smells came from people living together in unsanitary conditions. The occasional whiff of sewer water was enough to turn my stomach.

At this point I think my mom and my four sisters, especially the two older ones, started to worry a little. I guess it was not exactly the cleanest-looking place in the world. It most definitely wasn't anything like we had seen before and it must've been disconcerting for them to see all this squalor as we were driving to our new home.

It sure was an interesting drive, though. Wood carvings – of animals and ships mostly – were everywhere. Occasionally I'd see a rack of spears and swords for sale. Dad pointed out long black sticks adorned with brightly colored feathers. Those were blow guns, he said. That did it, I thought, I was staying.

Fortress House

We finally reached our new home. It was located in a small suburb of Angeles City where mostly Americans lived. Sure enough, our house had a wall around it, just like in dad's map. There was an iron gate on the driveway and in the back yard there was a large playhouse made of straw.

This was no regular straw hut. It was elevated up on four wooden stilts and it had a thatched roof. It was called a nipa hut. A perfect fort within a fort. Dad was sure going all out! We even got a new dog, named Charlie. Supposedly, Charlie, a German shepherd hybrid, flunked out of the huge K-9 training center at Clark because he was too good natured. It wouldn't do to have an attack dog slobbering all over people instead of biting them. I think Charlie flunked out because he was really a Filipino dog and he didn't understand English. Good natured dog though. He got along well with everyone; even the little cocker spaniel-poodle Aquarius we brought with us from Mississippi. It seemed Dad had thought of everything to make this a smooth transition for the family…or so he thought.

No sooner had we gotten in the house than my two older sisters began to cry, especially Donna, my oldest sister. The house was made of cinder blocks and you could tell, even from the inside. It was weird to have a room with cold brick walls. Worse, you couldn't drink the water from the tap because it was not clean enough. To top it all off, there were lizards in the house. I think the lizards pushed my sisters over the edge.

Lizards and Pigs

The lizards were called geckos. In my eyes, having them in the house was another plus for staying in the Philippines. Not to my sisters though. They would scurry about the walls and ceiling all the time and they would make this strange "geck-o" sound (the lizards, not my sisters). Hence the name, I imagine. The little guys sure were cute. Eventually, everybody grew to accept them in the house, even my sisters. Heck, I even stopped trying to capture them. After all, what was the point? They already lived in the house. Bigger lizards lived outside.

The huge and mighty chicken lizard grew as long as a foot and a half from head to tail. No small rubber-like gecko mouth here. Instead, they had a mouth full of jagged teeth. It wasn't called a chicken lizard because of its demeanor, only because of the way it sounded. They made a sound kind of like a chicken clucking. You could hear them off in the fields almost all the time, but they were rarely seen. They were elusive and very fast. If cornered, these lizards would lash out and bite you. Being bitten by a gecko was a lot like being chomped on by a gummy bear; being bitten by a chicken lizard was like getting attacked by a small alligator. So it was always a big deal when somebody actually captured a live chicken lizard – sort of like the big hunter returning from safari with a caged lion.

Our house backed up to an empty field across which lay a large culvert. At first I thought we lived near a river, but I quickly learned that it was nothing more than a large drainage ditch. On the opposite side lay a Filipino neighborhood. Occasionally, huge pigs would wander across the culvert and snort around our back wall. How cute, I thought, to have pigs nearby. (I can still hear my sisters complaining about those pigs.)

Dad warned me never to go back there. It was dangerous he said, plus the water in there was severely polluted. I wasn't even allowed to go back behind our wall, let alone go down into the ditch. He warned me those pigs could kill me.

I didn't quite believe him until one day a giant pig chased me up and out of the culvert. It wasn't until I got back over our wall that I stopped running. I didn't realize how big, mean, and fast those pigs were and, needless to say, I never went back there again, at least not by myself!

Water

One problem with our new house I never got used to: you couldn't drink the water from the tap. We had to drive all the way to the base, fill up jugs with clean water and bring it back. Sometimes I'd drive with Dad to the water station which looked and worked just like a stateside gas station. Instead of gas you got water; water clean enough for drinking and cooking. We would pull up to the station and fill up our five gallon jugs and head home. Eventually, the novelty wore off and going with Dad to refill the water jugs became boring. If I didn't know any better, I'd say it was a chore.

Not being able to drink the tap water was quite an experience. I remember how concerned I was about brushing my teeth. I asked Dad why we couldn't drink it. Bugs were in there, he said. I never could see any in the water, but before we left the Philippines I'd learn one horrific lesson: the bugs you can't see are generally the ones that would hurt you the most. However, the bugs you could see were by far the more interesting. There were huge spiders and all kinds of strange insects in the fields. At night the street lights would attract thousands of moths and beetles. So many interesting insects and spiders; especially the spiders...they were super aggressive.

Spider Fights

It was a neighborhood game to have spider fights and I remember watching in astonishment the first time I saw one. The spiders were captured and kept in a large matchbox which was modified with four compartments to house up to four spiders. When placed inside, the spiders would curl up into a ball and wait.

When challenged, two kids would hold a string or stick between them. Placing their champion spiders at the ends of the string or stick the spiders would race out to confront each other. A fierce battle would ensue as the spectators on both sides would ooh and aah. Rather quickly, one combatant would begin to dominate the other. The stronger one would wrap the loser into a ball of spider webbing and the contest was over. The winning spider owner had another victory under his belt and the loser had a neatly wrapped dead arachnid. It was something rather spectacular to watch.

My spiders never quite achieved heavy-weight status. I did

learn, though, that the longer the spiders stayed in the matchbox, the more aggressive they became. Looking back, I guess any starving animal would become more belligerent the longer it was deprived of food. As time passed, my interest in spider fighting waned. I had more fun tossing my starving spiders into a paper cup with a cockroach. The cockroaches never won. Eventually I gave up on catching spiders altogether…something more exciting would take their place. Something lying buried just underneath the surface; something far more interesting and dangerous than a half-starved spider. But that's another story, and one that will have to wait just a bit.

Sari-Sari

A couple of streets over was a neighborhood convenience store. I imagine a 1940s corner store looked a lot like this one. Mostly a wooden structure, this store had a wooden floor that creaked when you walked across it. It also had a take-your-time-and-look-around atmosphere. Most of the items which originally intrigued me about the Filipino lifestyle were commonplace here, like those stick brooms. And to top it all off, the prices were just right.

With just one American dollar you could buy a bottle of Pepsi, a handful of Bazooka Joe bubble gum, a couple of firecrackers, some matches and an assortment of small Filipino toys. But the most memorable thing about these stores were their names. They were called sari-sari (we pronounced it sorry-sorry) stores. I thought it was a joke. Eventually I came to rely on sari-sari stores no matter where I was in the Philippines. From Baguio City to Manila to the Subic Bay, sari-sari stores were everywhere.

Our New Life

Whatever inconveniences and oddities there were about our new life in the Philippines, I felt comfortable living there. That cinder block structure quickly became my home. From that house at night I could see fires burning in the sugar cane fields on the distant hills. The fires were set to help in the harvesting of the sugar cane. The ash would drift for miles and later fall upon the ground. During daylight hours, the ash falling looked a lot like snow falling. Inside our little fortress it was almost like we were still in America. We had a television, running water, beds, tables, even a kitchen.

Granted, we could not drink the water and the television had only one English-speaking station: the Armed Forces Philippine Network, more commonly known as AFPN. Or maybe the P stood for Pacific? Who knows. Anyway, I guess it was a plus to not watch any commercials which, in the traditional sense, did not exist on AFPN. There was nothing to advertise.

The Filipino stations had commercials. That's how I learned about San Miguel beer and White Castle whiskey – Filipino favorites. Instead, on AFPN, I learned the perils of perimeter guard duty on a large military installation and to never, ever remove your flight gloves during a jet refueling operation. The static electricity on your hands would spark the fuel, blowing you, the jet, and a large portion of the runway sky high. Handy information for an 11-year-old.

But the occasional gecko on the wall was always a reminder we weren't stateside. Outside of our home, the lumbering carabao (a water buffalo by any other name), the lush countryside, the vibrant green foliage and the warm, friendly attitude of the Filipinos wherever we went, was proof-positive we definitely weren't in the States.

When I went to bed at night, I felt safe and warm despite the cinder block walls. Except for Tony, my entire family was here. Even though armed guards patrolled the streets to enforce the curfews, I felt safe each night when I went to sleep.

-

CHAPTER 2

First Day of School

I had just begun the sixth grade before leaving Biloxi for the Philippines. Of the five schools at Clark Air Force Base, my school, for fifth and sixth grades was a pre-fabricated school located near a large hill covered with lush vegetation. The rise of ground behind the campus was called Lily Hill, and as such, was the name of the school.

I arrived at Lily Hill while classes were in session. After checking me in, I'll never forget my parents driving away, leaving me momentarily panicked and alone with a new teacher. As we walked through a maze of buildings, she explained that the school was very new. It was not hard to see: the buildings, sidewalks, and school playground were completely devoid of any surrounding vegetation – just a lot of sunbaked, tan-colored dirt. It was obvious the area had only been recently bulldozed. The school buildings, nothing more than mobile home-like structures, must have only just been assembled. It was in striking contrast to the hill behind the school.

The hill itself was covered with deep green-colored vegetation. The school yard ran right up against the base of it and stopped. Nothing, not even a fence, separated the playground from the jungle-covered terrain. But the entire hill was off limits I was told. Nobody was allowed to climb on it. I wondered why.

My first day of school started out uneventfully. I met my homeroom teacher and I liked most of my classmates right away. As a military brat it was important to learn how to make friends quickly. The alternative was loneliness. After school I went to catch the bus home, a little worried I'd miss it or get on the wrong one or something like that. It's amazing what kids worry about. Well, I got on the right one okay, but what a bus it was!

The School Bus

It wasn't like any other school bus I had ever seen before. It had the general shape of a typical stateside one, except it was not yellow; it was mostly red. Even more remarkable was it didn't have side windows. Instead, it had a thick, stiff, wire gauge screen stretched across where the windows would normally be. It was almost impossible to bend, even though the openings in the screen were big enough to put your fingers through. The urge to touch it was irresistible. Riding back and forth from school, I occasionally found myself clasping the screen with my entire hand. Presumably, it was to keep us from throwing things out of the window. However, years later, I learned those screens had another purpose. During the tumultuous years of Filipino martial law, Americans were often the targets of terrorism. A school bus full of American children was an inviting target. Strong, stiff screens provided protection from objects entering the bus from the outside, objects like rocks, sticks, cans, or even hand grenades. I heard rumors about Filipino rebels attacking the base and about American abductions. It just didn't seem likely to happen. At least not to me.

Bullets on the Ground

Being a little apprehensive that first day, I made sure I got to the right bus early, and as such I was one of the first kids on. Naturally, I took a window seat. Waiting for the other kids to board, I noticed a group of four or five boys all about my age, bending over and walking slowly through the playground. One or two even had their hands on their knees as they walked. The boys were looking for something. Other kids were running by or scrambling around, trying to get in one last swing, or turn down the slide, before having to go home. Curious, I watched these guys closely. Every once in a while they would pick something up, brush it off, put it in their pocket, and continue. They were oblivious to everything around them. I wondered what could be so interesting.

Finally, our bus was ready to go. One of the boys I had been watching looked up from the ground, dashed towards our bus, and scrambled on board just as the driver was shutting the door. The boy sat down across from me. I asked him what he was doing out there. He turned around, reached into his pocket and pulled out a handful of what looked like little rocks.

"Looking for these," he said. "They're bullets."

From that moment on I was hooked. At first I didn't understand, how could you find bullets on the playground? And these did not look like regular bullets, even though I had no idea what a real bullet looked like anyway. These were dark-colored and stained with tints of green. He let me hold them. They felt heavy and slightly cool to the touch. Some were real pointy and some were not, but all of them had scratches and dents. Some surface parts were particularly smooth. I rotated one around in my fingers as he started to talk about the war. It was like I was holding part of a treasure. Yeah, like pieces of gold from some pirate's treasure.

"What war?" I asked.

"World War II," he said. "The Japanese and Americans fought all over the base during World War II. One of the last and fiercest of all battles was the Battle of Lily Hill."

I couldn't believe it, but it was true. The Battle of Lily Hill, where our school was located, was the scene of some of the heaviest fighting between the Japanese and Americans during World War II. It was like I was in a time machine, racing back and forth between the past and the present. My only exposure to war, and World War II in particular, was through war movies and comic books. These bullets were my first tangible bit of evidence of a real war. Lily Hill was a real World War II battle ground.

The Legend of Lily Hill

The Battle of Lily Hill, according to my school bus scholar, was where the last stronghold of Japanese retreated to as the American and Filipino forces advanced on Clark Field (back when there was no such thing as an Air Force Base, just Army Air Corps Fields). The Japanese were notorious for not surrendering, preferring instead to fight to the death. Lily Hill was said to be infested with underground tunnels in which they hid. Around-the-clock air and artillery bombardments proved useless against the Japanese defenders buried deep in their bunkers. Large numbers of Americans were killed as they tried to take the hill. The situation was hopeless until, one night, a small group of Negritos broke the stalemate.

Negritos were indigenous to the Philippines long before any other peoples arrived from Polynesia and Malaysia. At 11 years of age I was taller than the tallest Negrito. They have a very dark, black complexion and are said to move like the wind across the plains. They are virtually undetectable once they enter the jungles and are renowned for their ability as trackers. Negritos helped America during the war, serving as both scouts and front line soldiers. Expert with both the bow and arrow and the blow gun, their strength and stamina were legendary. It was Negritos who, on one dark and moonless night, crept undetected through the Japanese lines on Lily Hill. By the next morning, a path had been cleared up one side of the hill. The Americans were able to storm up the breach in the lines and by the end of the day the battle was over. For their efforts the Negritos were forever granted special privileges on base, including free medical care at the base hospital. They were hired as base perimeter guards and worked with the U.S. military police in the protection and defense of all American property and personnel in the Philippine Islands. The Negritos at Clark lived in a tribal village of huts and shacks just outside the perimeter fence across the great basin plain past the flight line. As an American, I felt a sense of admiration and respect for the Negritos.

Because of the war, you could find bullets all over the place, you just had to look. Hundreds of thousands, perhaps even millions, of bullets were fired in anger. From watching war movies, it never dawned on me that those bullets had to end up somewhere. I definitely never thought I would be in a place where you could find them just lying around.

Well, actually it was not quite that easy. Anything just lying around was quickly picked up and hoarded by somebody, but every time a new road was built, or anything requiring the movement of dirt, it was inevitable that large amounts of ordnance would be found. Even the light construction and assembly of a pre-fabricated school resulted in a large cache of World War II stuff. And I do mean stuff. That kid on the bus told me if you looked long and hard enough, you could find rifles, bayonets, swords, pistols, canteens – just about anything. And the best time to scavenge around for bullets was right after it rained. Even a light rain would wash away a layer of topsoil, exposing a bunch of bullets. The story goes that shortly after the school was assembled, a heavy rain uncovered a long ago forgotten minefield exactly where the playground was planned! He said there were even undiscovered tunnels on Lily Hill, loaded with dead Japanese skeletons and tanks…the only problem was the booby-traps. Booby-traps! I thought. No wonder the hill was off-limits. Needless to say, it was an interesting ride home. I couldn't wait to get back to school tomorrow and look for bullets.

There was just one problem, I learned: collecting bullets was against the rules. Other kids on the bus confirmed it. Looking for them at school was against the law and possession could result in suspension. At first I could not understand why, it seemed harmless enough. But over time I began to learn otherwise. It was not until much later that I fully understood all those restrictions were for my own protection.

Unless you knew what you were doing, picking up a piece of ordnance could cause serious physical injury, blindness, baldness, or even death. Even something as harmless as a spent bullet head was potentially dangerous. Phosphorous, used to create tracer rounds, would burn once exposed again to air. Kids would find entire hand grenades, seemingly inert and harmless, the triggering mechanisms rusted solid over years of exposure. Not knowing any better, one thing would lead to another and playing army would suddenly turn into the real thing. Lily Hill was off-limits for a reason: unexploded ordnance was everywhere. It makes you wonder why a school was built so close to a major battlefield.

It took me a long time to figure it out, but World War II was a huge war. The Philippines, in particular the areas surrounding Clark Air Field, the Bataan Peninsula, and Manila Bay, were inundated with tons of weapons and ordnance from 1941 to 1945. Once a battle was fought, it was easy to lose things; rains would come quickly, vegetation would grow rapidly. The very landscape of the surface would change in a week or two's time.

Ammunition, helmets, rifles, bayonets, canteens, even large caliber artillery pieces, tanks, and airplanes were lost or misplaced. Tunnels built for defense were simply forgotten about once the war ended because the entrances had either caved in under attack or were hidden by thick vegetation. In time, it became impossible to start a construction project and not find World War II artifacts.

So in retrospect, it probably didn't matter where the school was placed. Scraping away the topsoil anywhere on base would have exposed some quantity of ordnance…not something your normal stateside school district would worry about.

EOD

The base did have a program to educate people, especially the younger ones, about the perils of unexploded ordnance. It was run by the EOD team (pronounced "E-O-D"), which stood for Explosive Ordnance Disposal. These units were manned with bomb experts.

As you might suspect, the EOD department at Clark was big. They actually had checkpoints on some parts of the base and "amnesty disposal boxes" were located in strategic places, like near the airport. The idea was for people to anonymously deposit ordnance they had in their possession. These drop boxes looked a lot like corner mail boxes, except they were covered with sandbags. The only exposed area was a little door through which you'd deposit your bullets and bombs.

The EOD unit would come to the schools and give talks, show films, and explain how looking for and finding ordnance was dangerous...and illegal. If you were caught with any in your possession, they'd take it away and you'd get in big trouble. I never really understood the big trouble part. I had heard stories about how they would raid houses and confiscate kids' bullets and bomb collections. It seemed like such a horrible thing to have spent all that time looking for and assembling a collection, only to have it snatched away without warning.

Only now, as an adult, am I able to comprehend the seriousness and danger associated with looking for those bullets. It was true some kids were seriously injured picking up this stuff. What a parent's nightmare. But as an 11-year-old riding the bus home on my first day of school, I came to an entirely different conclusion: looking for and collecting bullets was cool and the EOD was to be avoided at all costs. The EOD people were the bad guys.

I couldn't have been in the Philippines for more than a couple of weeks and already I was dreaming of finding a long-lost Japanese tunnel full of rifles and tanks. Once I found it, I had no intention of sharing it with the EOD unit. I couldn't wait to explore that hill.

Elephant Grass

As the months rolled by, my new life in the Philippines began to settle down. All the things that at first were so interesting began to seem commonplace, mostly because it was so commonplace. My bullet collection was indeed growing, but finding them around the school yard was getting pretty boring. Even my few excursions up and onto Lily Hill were uneventful. Not only that, but it required a great deal of effort to sneak up the hill. Escaping from the school yard to the base of the hill was easy enough, because once you moved into the bamboo groves and other tall grasses, you were generally undetectable from observers down below. But that was the problem – it was difficult to move through that stuff. Bamboo grows in clusters and it was almost impossible to get through a cluster without a machete or bolo which, unfortunately none of us kids ever seemed to have on hand. If a bamboo grove was in your way, valuable time had to be wasted going around it. Equally distressing was the elephant grass.

Elephant grass was tall, green grass. It was beautiful, really. From a distance, a field of elephant grass would gracefully sway from side-to-side with the wind. Its motion would seem so fluid, it reminds me today of a seabed of kelp moving back-and-forth with the waves. Up close, the grass looked just like the common grasses found in most lawns back home in the states, only larger. Elephant grass would grow as high as six feet tall. Hence the name.

Now as most of us know, the grass growing in most stateside lawns is pleasant to walk on, even when you're barefoot. You'd kind of expect the same thing by looking at a field of elephant grass. No luck, though. This grass had hideously sharp edges that would slice up any exposed skin it came in contact with. Wearing a short-sleeved shirt and walking into a field of elephant grass would result in multiple paper-like cuts and contusions up and down your arms. If you were wearing shorts, forget it. And once you got into a field of it, unless you were well over six feet tall, you had no idea where you were going. None of us could see through it or over it. I think the furthest we ever made it through elephant grass was maybe ten feet before giving up and looking for an alternate route.

Sometime later, when I was in the Boy Scouts, my dad and my patrol climbed a large hill not too far from our house. It was covered almost entirely with elephant grass. Before long, the patrol had started to give up hope of ever reaching the top.

My dad, however, was never one to give up easily. With a little ingenuity, he came up with a plan. With no machete to cut our way through, he turned around and with his back facing the grass, simply fell down. We would pull him up and then stomp the bent grass flat. Dad would then walk a few feet forward and repeat the process. At some places the grass was so thick, Dad could not fall back on his own so we had to actually push him back until the grass would collapse under us. Eventually we reached the top. What a day that was.

Unfortunately, I couldn't bring my dad along with me as I was sneaking up Lily Hill looking for World War II contraband, not that it would have helped. There were no bare spots on the hill at all. The vegetation was just too thick. With all that ground cover, it was impossible to find anything unless we stepped on it, which was unlikely.

We did find a few caves, but no tunnels. Each cave we found would raise our hopes that this was the one, the mother lode – a hidden army lay just around the corner. The caves we found were really nothing more than small holes dug into the sides of the hill. I think the biggest one only went back maybe 10 to 15 yards. We never found anything of any value in those caves, either. Worse, all we ever seemed to find in those caves were discarded Coke or Pepsi bottles; evidence, it would seem, that we weren't the first people to discover these places. It was disappointing to think we could find more stuff right around the school playground than up on the hill.

Snakes

But I never gave up on Lily Hill. Sneaking up there was half the fun; rambling around in the foliage was the other half. We were always afraid of the dreaded booby traps, but we were most definitely terrified of the snakes.

Snakes were everywhere it seemed – or so I heard. I don't actually remember seeing many wild ones. I guess it's the one or two you do see that stick out in your mind the most. Of course, as kids, especially young boys, we tended to exaggerate in our own minds the reality of the snakes. My biggest fear was to come face-to-face with a spitting cobra or the mysterious two-step snake which, as everybody knows, would leave you alive just long enough for you to take two steps before you fell down dead. I never saw any snakes on Lily Hill, but that is not to say they weren't there. Snakes were all over the place and some of them were very dangerous.

I'll never forget our first New Year's Eve spent in the

Philippines. We were still living off-base in our fortress house. Earlier that day, I cut my foot while running barefoot through a field between our house and the sari-sari store. I was buying firecrackers for the night.

The cut on my foot was pretty severe and it required a trip to the hospital along with several stitches. It also required a tetanus shot. Outbreaks of tetanus were not uncommon in the Philippines, but as you know, I hated shots. I did, however, learn never to run around barefoot again, at least not off base, where most fields in Angeles City were strewn with debris. That evening, my foot was all bandaged up and I couldn't walk on it at all. My destiny for the night was to lay around in the house (I never did figure out what happened to my firecrackers), while the rest of the family could go outside and enjoy the New Year festivities…all except for Dad.

Dad had been working a swing shift at the hospital before coming home late that evening while I was in the living room playing a game with a neighborhood friend; everyone else was outside somewhere. Dad walked in and asked me if I could hear the barking dog in our backyard. He seemed incredulous that nobody but him could hear it. He was worried some rabid stray dog had gotten into our backyard. Rabies were a big deal at the time. Several neighborhood kids had been exposed to the disease since we had been there. It seemed like I was always meeting some poor soul on the bus who was undergoing treatment for rabies. And for me, anyway, the rabies treatment seemed particularly brutal: multiple shots in the stomach. My forehead would begin to sweat whenever I would even think about it.

Dad grabbed a flashlight and a broom, and quietly mumbling to himself about how deaf everybody must be, went out to investigate. I just lay there of course, too wounded to move. Seconds later the door flew open and Dad, who only moments ago was calm, had a look of terror on his face.

"There's a huge snake in our yard!" he shouted.

It seemed everybody in the neighborhood was instantly alerted. Our across-the-street neighbor's wiener dog had apparently cornered a large python in our backyard. I imagine after accidentally slithering over our wall, the poor snake was probably pretty dazed and confused when confronted with this small, yet incredibly noisy creature. Using his keen sense of smell, the wiener dog probably thought he was keeping the world safe for democracy. In reality, he was probably only a few seconds from certain death.

I really hated having the bandage on my foot. Capturing the snake quickly became a major event; an event I was unable to directly participate in. I couldn't even hop outside. All the information I was receiving, at best, was second hand. It was annoying.

The first attempt at capturing the snake, or so I heard, failed when the bamboo pole used to lift the snake cracked and splintered under the snake's weight. This evidently was a big reptile. Eventually, the snake was lifted and placed inside a large trash can.

The next morning, I got my first glimpse of the python. Dad had removed the trash can lid and placed a piece of very stiff screen across the opening, which had been securely fastened down. Good thing, too. Once I eased myself up to the can, I moved my head over the opening to peer down upon the snake. It was indeed a big one. And fast.

The snake – suddenly and without warning – struck up at the screen with blinding speed. The force with which it hit the screen caused the trash can to rock. It happened so fast that by the time I jumped back, the snake had already figured out he was not going to break through. I didn't poke my head over the opening again, but I did get a pretty good look at him the first time. He was so big and long he had to curl around himself several times just to lie there, completely covering the bottom of the trash can in the process. He was a handsome brown snake, with beautiful diamond shaped patterns along his thick body. Poor thing must have hurt his nose on the screen; he was probably still mad about letting the wiener dog get away.

Dad and some of the other kids were going to bring our snake to the Jungle Survival School on base. This was the first I heard of that school, but it certainly would not be the last. As the name implies, the school was a place where one would go to learn how to survive in a jungle. An education facility mainly for pilots and aircrew members, it was required training for anybody flying over to Vietnam. It was located way out past the flight line in a pretty much unpopulated area of the base. A large facility, the campus had several buildings used as classrooms, a man-made jungle covering several acres, helicopter landing sites, and a zoo. Well, it wasn't a real zoo in the normal sense, and it wasn't usually open to the public. The whole purpose of the place was to better prepare people for jungle survival behind enemy lines. It was important to know what to do and especially what not to do in the jungle; like what kind of plants you could or could not eat and what kind of animals to avoid, particularly the slithering kind. On top of all that, it was important to learn how to remain undetected by the enemy and to eventually be rescued. That's called survival, escape, evasion, and rescue; not a simple feat. To that end, the Jungle Survival School had a small zoo containing hundreds of snakes, lizards, birds, wild pigs and even some alligators.

The school seemed the logical place to bring our captured snake. After all, we had to do something with it. I guess we could have kept it as a pet, but what would we feed it? I knew of only one wiener dog in our neighborhood and my little brother and sisters were probably just a little too big for it to swallow...at least not without anybody noticing.

I didn't get to go along to drop off our snake at the school, but heard all about it. Our snake was identified as an Indian Python, a snake very common to the Philippines. He measured just under 10 feet long! The school already had an Indian Python, but they took ours anyway. Their snake was named Charlie - same name as our dog. Come to think of it, the whole time I was in the Philippines I never met a real person named Charlie; just animals.

Charlie the Snake

Charlie the snake had been around for years. He was bigger and fatter than our snake, almost 15 feet long. They fed him live chickens about once a month. The school people must have thought two snakes would be better than one and twelve extra chickens a year probably seemed well worth the price. Well, they didn't have to worry; within a month's time, we learned Charlie the Snake had eaten our snake. Either he didn't want to share his chickens or he was just plain tired of eating chickens all the time. Whatever the reason, I felt pretty responsible for our snake's death.

A few years later I got a chance to see Charlie the Snake. He was being moved to Subic Bay's survival school because Clark's school was closing. I can still picture him in my mind: big and fat. I assumed he was so big because he was a caged snake. I never believed a wild snake could get as big as old Charlie…at least, not until a few years later.

While I was attending Wagner Middle School, a cobra wandered onto campus. Curious students unintentionally cut off the animal's escape route to the jungle. The snake was backed into a corner by the time I arrived on the scene. Frightened and surrounded by kids who didn't know any better, the cobra raised his head and flared his neck. What a terrifying, yet beautiful sight. Its skin was a dark green color. Fearing for the safety of the students, the snake was shot and killed. Stretched out along the ground, it measured over 15 feet long! Some parts of the cobra were as big around as my leg. I heard some people say they found a partially digested wiener dog in his stomach. One thing I do know for sure, that cobra would have given old Charlie the Snake a run for his money.

The Perimeter

Our family's name eventually reached the top of the base housing list and we moved into a beautiful ranch style house on 87th Place. Unlike our place off base, there was no wall surrounding the yard, not even a fence. My mom liked the house because it had central air conditioning. It also had the added benefit of clean, drinkable water, right from the tap. Sometimes they suspected something would go wrong and an alert would be issued to fill the bathtubs up with water as a contingency. Just in case, the water in the bathtubs would become our emergency drinking water supply. Alerts like that usually preceded the arrival of tropical typhoons.

Typhoons would drop tons of water on the countryside within a relatively short period of time and drainage ditches would become raging rivers within minutes. It was not uncommon for the base water processing plant to become deluged with contaminated water. I was always drawn to the drainage ditches during the rainstorms. The fast moving water was fascinating – and dangerous. I heard about kids being swept away into the underground pipes, only to be found dead a few days later. Never saw that happen to anyone though.

I liked our new house because of its location. Behind it, and to the left, were more houses. But directly behind, and to the right of it, was the perimeter road, which as the name implies, was a road that ran the entire length of the base just inside the fence line. Needless to say, it was a very long road.

The perimeter road was neat. Just on the other side stood a chain-link fence topped with barbed wire: the perimeter fence. Beyond lay some of the most beautiful countryside I've ever seen; it was as if we lived on the edge of a great, green valley. Mountains bordered the opposite side.

Our yard was kind of neat, too; we even had a mango tree. But the perimeter road drew most of my attention. Every quarter mile or so stood a guard tower which was really just a covered platform raised up on four long telephone poles and which were normally manned by Negritos. They wore gray fatigues and were armed with 12-gauge shotguns and occasionally you'd see one on foot patrol along the road. Sometimes jeeps or trucks would drive by, but traffic along the road was generally light and restricted to security vehicles. On our side, I felt safe and secure; on the opposite side lay the badlands...or so I imagined.

At first it was unclear to me what the fence and road were for. Obviously it was there to keep something out, but what? Except for the occasional farmers walking by with their carabao, I never saw anybody else out there. It was kind of eerie actually. The few times I saw any farmers, they always seemed to walk by in single file and they almost never spoke, at least not to us. If the farmers did speak, they spoke Tagalog with hushed voices. The people on the other side would usually just stare at us as they went by. As quickly as they appeared, they would be gone. I used to play along the perimeter road quite a bit, nobody ever seemed to mind. Heck, the Negrito guards would even let me up into the towers once and awhile, just to look around. What a view!

"Robbed!"

One day Dad noticed our trash cans were missing. We were told they had probably been stolen and we should keep them chained up from now on. I laughed when I heard that theory. Who would steal trash cans? The sad part was it was true; they were stolen.

The Philippines was, and still is, an incredibly poor country. The majority of the people worked hard all day long and still remained impoverished. Off-base we had a nipa hut in our backyard which we used as a playhouse. A lot of Filipinos actually lived in nipa huts. An aluminum trash can, when cut down the side and rolled flat, served nicely as a huge roof tile, much better at keeping rain out than a thatched roof would. The farmers who walked along the fences and saw our homes, yards, roads, and schools must have thought we were the richest people in the world. Many Filipinos didn't even have indoor plumbing and yet we were using precious metal to hold our trash. I was beginning to understand why they'd stare at us from across the perimeter fence.

Once, we really were robbed. It was late at night and Mom heard one of our dogs, Aquarius, barking. Actually, mom said she only heard one bark; Aquarius was a pretty laid-back dog. Mom got up to investigate. Looking out from the kitchen window into our carport, she was startled to see several shadowy figures. The alarm was quickly sounded. I was awakened by Mark as he grappled with a three-foot long ceremonial sword Dad had bought in Thailand.

"We're being robbed!" Mark exclaimed as he ran out the door.

I hurried down from the top bunk bed. Not to be out-done, I reached for a finely crafted knife we had picked up in Germany. Actually, it was only a letter opener; however, I wasn't about to leave the room unarmed. David, my youngest brother, was just now regaining consciousness.

I repeated, "We're being robbed," and I, too, dashed away. Running outside, I was quickly swept up in the excitement of the moment. It was very late and dark outside…that in itself was cool. Then to see Mom and Dad outside, along with the rest of the family, jumping up and down and shouting for help, was even cooler. Dad was getting frustrated because he couldn't get the attention of the guard in the tower. He even stopped yelling, "Help! We've been robbed," and started yelling, "Help! Were on fire!" just to get somebody's attention. He thought out loud that we had been robbed by somebody working in cahoots with the guard in the tower. Mark, still brandishing his weapon, had moved up to the perimeter fence to get a closer look. There, for all the world to see, was a huge hole cut in the fence. Part of it had been peeled back and wired into place. It looked almost like a door. And sure enough, our bikes and garbage cans were gone.

Alongside the hole, just inside the fence, were three or four pairs of shoes. The shoes were aligned neatly in a row. It would seem our robbers were on the run in their bare feet. Why they took the time to put their shoes in a neat little row has always been a mystery. I always imagined if I ever were to meet them, I would find myself face-to-face with a bunch of polite robbers.

By the time the security police arrived, I assumed the burglars would be far away. A flare was quickly popped off. Interestingly enough, we could still see the robbers in the distance, across the fence, and way down into the valley. They were carrying their ill-gotten wares on their backs. All I could think was there go all our bikes; most importantly, my bike. I loved that bike.

Then, inexplicably, the robbers just dropped everything and disappeared into the darkness and sometime later we got our stuff back. What an adventure that was. Good thing I didn't have to use my letter opener…somebody could have gotten hurt.

"Mayday! Mayday!"

Not every day was as exciting as the day we were robbed. Some days I remember being flat-out bored, a situation which usually preceded me getting into trouble. Once, I was sitting in my room, trying to do homework. Outside my window I saw my younger brother, David, and one of his friends as they were playing with walkie-talkies. I had an idea and quickly broke out my own walkie-talkies. Actually, I think they were Tony's old set of walkie-talkies. I wasn't supposed to be using them, but I figured it would be all right just this one time.

Giggling almost uncontrollably, I turned one on and was delighted when I could hear both Dave and his friend chattering away on my handset. Then, in my best pilot voice, I proceeded to send out a "Mayday, Mayday" distress call. Watching from the window, I could see both Dave and his friend gasp in amazement and scurry about in confusion. I was almost rolling in tears at my cleverness, when all of a sudden, a grown up voice came crackling over the speaker. Talk about instant fear. This guy was asking for the mayday caller to keep "keying his mike" so he could "vector in a rescue" helicopter or something like that. I don't think I ever put away anything as fast in my life. Almost as soon as I had heard that guy, I was back at my desk studying. Excitedly, David and his friend came running in to tell everybody about what they had heard. Luckily, I don't think anybody believed them and I sure wasn't about to confirm their story. I was positive whoever the guy was, he was "vectoring" the security police to my house to arrest me.

It was little episodes like the walkie-talkie fiasco which I liked best. Living in a faraway tropical land did have its advantages. Even though I would get bored, it wasn't hard to find something cool to do.

Falling Trees

Once, I was at school registering for classes with my mom. A tremendously loud crash came from the parking lot. Whatever had just happened, it sounded like it broke a lot of glass and metal. The crashing sounds were accompanied by a small temblor. At first I thought it was an earthquake. We had quite a few earthquakes in the Philippines, but never any real big ones. Never, ever did we have any with loud noises.

Running outside, I was awed by the sight of several cars

crushed beneath the weight of a huge tree. There was no wind and it was not raining; the tree just fell down, probably from old age. Nobody was hurt, but there amidst the wreckage were dead or dying snakes and lizards on the pavement. Apparently caught off guard, these animals just fell to their deaths. One lizard was especially large and beautiful, even though it was dead. It was a large iguana-type lizard with a deep emerald green color along most of its body. I never even knew those lizards lived in the Philippines, and for as long as I lived there, I never saw another one like it.

Layover in Saigon

It was hard for me to remember the passage of time like we did in Mississippi since we didn't have North American-type seasons. There were no autumns or winters to speak of and the closest thing to a springtime was the rainy season. I guess the summertime was marked with the passing of the dry season. Those two seasons were easy to remember.

If it was raining, it was usually the rainy season and if it was hot and not raining, it was probably the dry season. With that kind of set-up, one just didn't need to look at a calendar. Doing so would have only made things worse since every six months I had to get booster shots...cholera and typhoid booster shots! It was like having this big hammer hanging over my head that never went away, yet time would march on and then - bam! - there it was to smack me in the head, or, more appropriately, stick me in the arm. The anticipation of the shots was always distressing; the sharp pain and accompanying numbness was downright irritating. The numbness was actually so bad that you could always count on someone in the family to accidentally drop a plate or glass.

Once, right after we had our shots, Dad brought the five youngest children to the swimming pool. He said if we exercised our arms the numbness would not be as severe. So, we all joined the Clark Air Force Base swim team, the Flying Dolphins. I don't think any of us knew how to swim, but somehow we managed.

It wasn't long before swimming became a big part of my

life. Going to practice and attending meets became regularly scheduled events. We went to meets in Manila and at Subic Bay. Once, we even went to a swimming meet in Bangkok, Thailand. We "hopped" over there on a C-5 military transport plane. On the way back we had a layover in Saigon, Vietnam. There were four of us: me, Dad, David (my youngest brother) and Cindy (my second-to-the-oldest sister).

While in Saigon waiting for our connecting flight back to the Philippines, our seats were bumped. Well, actually only one seat was bumped. I remember standing next to my dad up at the flight operations counter while some airman was explaining there were only three seats available. Simple math told me one of us had to stay behind. I had a sinking suspicion it was going to be me.

I knew there was a war going on in Vietnam, it was pretty obvious just by standing in the terminal. Heavily armed soldiers were milling about the place. Outside, sandbags, jeeps, and armored vehicles were everywhere. I have to admit; it was kind of cool actually…but also a little scary. I also knew things were not going smoothly for the Americans in Southeast Asia. People were being killed there, but as long as Dad was around I didn't mind being in this country. Heck, I wouldn't even mind spending a night or two. But now, I was beginning to get genuinely frightened that Dad was going to take those last seats to Clark and leave me there to fend for myself.

I heard Dad say to the airman that he really had to get back. Surely he wouldn't leave one of us behind, would he? As I stood there next to him, he reached out and placed his hand on my head. That meant he was preparing to tell me the bad news, I thought. This was not looking good as I saw Dad stare silently at the airman behind the counter. Then he slowly turned to me and gave me the "Don't worry son, you'll be okay" look. Now I was really, really worried. Oh no, I thought, this is it as Dad turned to face the airman again. With an exaggerated sigh, Dad said he had better wait for the next flight out. What a relief!

You never realize how much you rely on your parents until you are confronted with the possibility of being without them. I didn't stray more than a couple of feet from Dad until we got back home in the Philippines. Dad couldn't even use the bathroom by himself; I wasn't going to take any chances that he might sneak away.

The Crossbow

Besides swimming, school, snakes, and shots, there was the Bamboo Bowl, a local putt-putt golf, and lots of other stuff to occupy our time. The Bamboo Bowl was the base stadium where high school games and other outdoor events and celebrations were held, including the "Happening on the Green," more commonly known as the HOG.

The HOG was the equivalent of the country fair, except with a Filipino flair. I got my first crossbow at the HOG. I bought it from a Negrito for about 16 pesos, which was roughly one American dollar. It had to be one of the neatest weapons I ever laid my hands on. Unfortunately, I lost all my arrows within a week trying to shoot birds and other animals while hunting around the perimeter road. Thank goodness I never shot anybody, let alone actually hit any animals. Once an arrow landed across the perimeter fence, it might as well have landed on the moon – there was just no way for me to get the arrows back.

All my attempts at making my own arrows proved futile. I tried making them from bamboo shafts, sticks, and darts. I soon lost patience and eventually just gave up on it altogether. Besides, I got tired of sneaking around with the crossbow…I wasn't supposed to have it in the first place.

CHAPTER 3

A Boring Saturday

One day not long after we moved on base, I remember being really bored. It was on a Saturday, I think. I found myself all alone, swinging on the playground at Grissom Elementary School. The school, for third and fourth grades, was just right down the hill from where we lived on 87th Place and was named after one of the original seven American astronauts. He was killed along with two other astronauts in a fire on the Apollo 1 rocket.

There I was, just swinging away, when along came this red-headed kid carrying a big paper bag. He was about as tall as me and obviously about the same age. I can't remember his name exactly, but I think it was Jim. Being new on base, I asked him what there was to do around here. He replied "not much" and added there were not many kids our age who lived right around the school. Besides, it was still pretty early in the morning. In fact, he said, he didn't even live around here himself; he lived down in one of the barns.

The barns were big, huge houses which pre-dated World War II and were located next to the parade field, way down on another part of the base. They looked like the kind of barn you would find on a typical Midwestern farm. Even though they were old houses, my mom wanted to live in one because they were so big. Some had five to six bedrooms; just perfect for a family of ten. During the Japanese occupation of the base in World War II, Japanese soldiers lived in the barns. That's why on some nights you could hear their haunted ghosts stumbling around and speaking Japanese – or so I heard.

I asked Jim what he was doing so far from home and how he got over here; after all, it was a long way from the barns. He said he walked. The school was located in the shadow of a small mountain, but being at a lower elevation than our house, neither the school nor the mountain peak could be seen from our home. The school lay almost at the base of the mountain except for a large depression that separated the school yard from the bottom of the mountain, which actually lay off the base. Running straight through the depression was the perimeter road. Standing in the playground and looking down, you could just barely see the perimeter fence. Nothing stood between the playground and the perimeter road except a field of short, green grass which sloped gently down. Looking straight across and up stood the mountain. It was indeed a beautiful sight.

The mountain was always covered in a blanket of green and parts of it were terraced for farming. Standing there gazing at the mountain, it looked deceptively small. It wasn't until Jim pointed to the farmers walking along a trail that I realized just how big the mountain was. Except for these five farmers, nobody else could be seen. As they were making their way down from the terraces to the bottom, Jim explained why he was here. He said he came up to do some trading; he was going to trade old clothes for weapons.

My eyes widened. Old clothes for weapons? Did I just die and go to heaven? Jumping off the swing, I excitedly asked him to explain the details. He said the farmers would find bullets, guns, helmets, and bayonets all the time as they worked the fields. To the farmers it was useless junk. It literally had no value; it was more of a nuisance than anything else. They couldn't eat it or wear it, and it was illegal to sell it. There was, however, a black market for these items, but the only people who shopped at it were Americans.

Jim was here to trade some of his old clothes and shoes for weapons. He showed me what he had in his bag: an old pair of shoes, a pair of pants, a couple of shirts and even some old underwear. He said underwear traded very well for some reason.

Trading at the Perimeter

My head was swimming. I asked if I could tag along. Jim said it was okay and so we headed down towards the perimeter fence together. By the time we reached the road, the farmers were waiting on the other side of the fence. Sure enough, they had a lot of stuff with them, including an old Thompson machine gun and a rather large bayonet.

It was the first real Japanese bayonet I had ever seen and I was drawn to it immediately. I had to have it. Jim was having his own private conversation with two or three of the farmers, trying to barter his clothes for the machine gun. I, on the other hand, was trying desperately to think of something I could trade for the bayonet. Remembering what Jim had told me earlier, I was even thinking of pulling my pants off and tossing my underwear over the fence.

I found a one-dollar bill in my pocket. Excitedly, I offered it up for trade; I thought for sure the man with the bayonet would take it. One American dollar was worth a considerable amount of money on the Filipino exchange market. Much to my disappointment, he didn't exactly jump at the offer. Instead, he kept asking me in very bad and broken English if I had any coins. Apparently, he either wasn't familiar, or didn't feel comfortable, with paper money. He wanted coins.

It was like hooking a big fish and reeling it in only to watch it drop back into the water and swim away. Obviously contemplating the offer, he wanted to look at the dollar before he would trade. I said it'd be okay only if I could look at the bayonet. No way was I going to be ripped off. Agreeing to my demand, he let me hold the bayonet blade as it was sticking through the chain link fence, but with the handle on his side of the fence. As the man was carefully examining my dollar bill, I stood there like an idiot with my hand on an 18-inch bayonet blade. All he had to do was grab the handle and pull the bayonet back through the fence. If I tried to hold onto the blade, my hand would have been cut. I was embarrassed by how stupid I must have looked.

For lack of a better plan, I just continued to stand there and hoped nobody would notice my stupidity. Eventually, the man with the bayonet reached a decision and handed the money back. My heart sank as he began shaking his head from side-to-side, signifying no deal. Jim wasn't having much luck, either. He became more and more frustrated with not being able to reach an agreement on the Thompson.

The Trap

Finally, one of the farmers suggested we move our discussion on down the perimeter road. Judging by how the others treated him, this guy seemed to be the leader of the group. His name was Pete. He was dressed a lot like the Filipino I had seen when I first stepped off the airplane a year ago. He was about as tall as I was and was wearing a machete at his side. He talked more than anyone in the group, probably because he had the best English. Pete seemed like a happy guy; always smiling and laughing a lot.

We couldn't have walked farther than a quarter of a mile, but what a difference a thousand feet or so can make. As we walked, I failed to notice the perimeter road gradually sloping further and further down in between the mountain and the base. The mountain was still very visible, but the school and guard tower could no longer be seen. On the base side, the field of short, green grass had gradually been replaced by a thick, densely-packed patch of jungle.

Eventually we stopped at a place where the perimeter fence had fallen down. Now we can get down to some serious trading, I thought, as things should go a lot quicker without the fence in the way. Pete stepped across first and approached Jim, and the both of them began to barter again as Pete was nonchalantly holding the bayonet in his left hand. The farmer I had unsuccessfully tried to trade with must have given it to Pete earlier as they had moved down the fence line. I watched them for a second, just a little bummed that the bayonet was probably going to be traded away for some clothes and not my dollar bill. Then something weird happened; something which I'll never forget for as long as I live.

Warnings

One of my greatest comic book heroes of all time was, and still is, Spiderman. As a kid, I often day-dreamed about how neat it would be to have his incredible spider powers. One of his trademark super powers was the famous "spider sense," or his ability to sense danger before it happened. Spiderman's tingling sixth sense had saved him on countless occasions.

At this moment, just like Spiderman, I could feel a tingling sensation warning me of impending danger. Looking back after all these years, I think it was more the hair raising on the back of my neck, accompanied by a terrifying chill running down my spine. I'm obviously not Spiderman, but standing there at that moment, I could feel that something bad was about to happen…and it did.

Suddenly Pete reached up and very quickly and violently grabbed Jim's arm. Aiming the tip of the bayonet straight at Jim's throat, Pete, through clenched teeth, asked "Do you want to die?" He was no longer smiling and instead was staring intently into Jim's face, determined it seemed to kill him no matter what the reply. Jim, frozen with fear, understandably had a look of sheer terror on his face.

Behind me, both to the right and left, stood two of the other men who by this time had quietly positioned themselves between me and the jungle. A fourth man stood on the perimeter road, blocking the route back up from which we came, and the fifth man was still standing on the other side of the fence. When Pete grabbed Jim, I could see from the corners of my eyes the two men behind me…as they started to move towards me.

The way we came was blocked. Pete, still holding Jim, stood between me and the other way down the road and there was no way I was going to run off base. I stood there for what seemed like an eternity. In reality, it couldn't have been more than a second or two. I had to do something.

The Chase

To this day, I'll never truly know how I got past those two guys behind me. It's possible Pete made his move too soon, catching them both off guard, or they just weren't anticipating me to react as quickly or to run in the direction I did. Whatever the reason, I just blew past those two guys as fast as I could and literally leapt into the jungle behind them

Now this particular patch of jungle was on base and I knew there was a road on the other side. Somewhere. If I could just make it to the road, I thought, I'd be safe. That was the good news. Of course, there was one problem, and it was a big one. I knew from my experiences on Lily Hill that jungles were difficult to move through. To make matters worse, I realized we had been led into a trap and there was a great possibility no one had seen Jim and me go down that road. Unless I made it all the way through the jungle there'd be no help…for either of us.

I'm sure the fear of it all was a big player, but moving off the perimeter road and into the jungle seemed as if I had instantly moved from a world of light into a surreal world of darkness. Standing on the road, the sky was big and blue, and the sun was simply dazzling. You could feel the sunlight as it hit your skin. Jumping into the jungle, I immediately felt surrounded. It was still hot, but the sun seemed to have disappeared. Out on the perimeter you could almost taste the dirt from the road in the air; in the jungle, it seemed as if I had slammed into a wall of dampness.

Whatever I was feeling, I was being driven by fear as I moved through the foliage as quickly and as straight as possible. In my panic, I was afraid of getting disoriented and running around in a circle and ending back out on the road I just left. I remember momentarily being afraid of running into a snake, but that fear was quickly forgotten.

As I ran, I thought I could hear somebody behind me. Crashing through a jungle is incredibly noisy and whether or not I was hearing the sounds of my own footsteps or the sounds of somebody else's just inches behind me did not matter. I wasn't going to look back; I just ran faster.

I burst into a small clearing and there before me appeared to be a trail which had been cut into the jungle. At first it wasn't apparent what had made the path, but I was able to quickly deduce that it wasn't a path at all. Instead, it was a very shallow culvert and it had water in it. I remember thinking that could be bad, but didn't stop for a second as I stepped down into the water. Initially I was afraid of slipping or getting stuck in some mud. Fortunately, it wasn't even ankle-deep and the bed was somewhat firm. I splashed across in about four steps at breakneck speed. Just as quickly as I had come upon the water, I was past it and back up into the jungle on the opposite side with no problem.

The Holes

Then something strange began to happen. The ground I was running across was sinking in places. But there was no water. Instead, there were holes – big holes – which appeared to be large enough for me to fall into…and there were a lot of them. Fortunately, a very thick layer of grasses had spread out across the jungle floor covering them. The grass mesh was acting as a safety net as I ran across them. But the holes were a mystery: Where did they come from? How deep were they? I couldn't see the holes beneath the grass until I was right on top of them, so it was difficult to avoid them. At least not without slowing down, which was out of the question. As I continued running, I could feel myself sinking down into and then out of them. I was absolutely terrified of becoming trapped in one and being caught, but as rapidly as they appeared in my path, the holes were gone. I began to feel like I was winning the race.

I blasted out of the jungle and back into the sunlight with a tremendous sense of relief. I could see the road ahead. The only thing between me and it was a field of short, mowed grass. The road couldn't have been more than 50 yards away. Nothing was stopping me now. To my left, about a quarter of a mile or more away, I could see the Grissom school yard. There wasn't a person in sight. I reached the road feeling like an Olympic champion. Without breaking stride, I ran right into the street. From where I was standing, cars coming from either direction would have had plenty of time to see me, at least in theory. I have no idea what the speed limit was on that particular stretch of highway, but I doubt it was over 35 mph.

I didn't have to wait long. Within seconds I could see a car approaching. I jumped up and down and waved my arms frantically as the car slowed down and stopped. For as scared as I was, I remember thinking for a moment how I had always wanted to do that. An airman, wearing green fatigues got out. Before he could even ask my anything, I ran up to him and started crying hysterically. No matter how hard I tried, I just couldn't verbally communicate anything of value to him as I collapsed in his arms. I remember seeing the airman look back towards the jungle. For the first time, I looked back as well. Nobody was coming. Seeing nothing, the airman put me in his car and drove to the nearest telephone, which was at someone's house.

Help

The airman explained to the dad of the house what had happened; namely that he saw me run from the jungle into the road, scream something about kidnappers, and collapse in his arms. They called the security police while the mom of the house tried her best to comfort me. I just sat there in a chair, shaking, until the security police arrived. I can't explain how good it felt to see those guys show up, it was like having the cavalry arrive. One guy was wearing a blue uniform and carrying a service revolver on his belt. The other security policeman was wearing fatigues; he looked so much more dangerous than the first…mainly because he was shouldering an M-16 rifle equipped with a grenade launcher.

The bad news was I knew these guys. They had picked me and some of my friends up about a month ago for trespassing and they remembered who I was (that's another story). Fortunately, they didn't hold it against me. When they asked me what had just happened, I found myself blathering like a baby again. They could tell by my uncontrollable crying and shaking that something bad had happened and decided they wanted to go down and see where all this had occurred. That scared me, but they convinced me I'd be okay with them in their vehicle.

It was a big truck with a cool camouflage paint job. I sat in the middle as we drove over to the school and then down onto the perimeter road. They commented about the tower being empty and one of them radioed in for somebody to come out and man it for a while. We slowly drove down into the area where I last saw Jim. I was a little nervous, but it was comforting to be snuggled in between all that firepower as they radioed in about the fence being down. Listening to the radio was neat. Then and now, there's just something cool about radio chatter.

Then, the security policeman with the grenade launcher said he saw three Filipino guys standing off to the right, just across the fence. I saw them too. The security policeman dressed in blue asked me if I recognized any of them; but by this time, we had already driven past their location. The security policeman in blue said he would turn around so I could get a better look, but by now, the people on the other side of the fence were gone. It was spooky.

What scared me even worse was when the security policeman with the grenade launcher expressed his concern to "get the hell out of there," as he chambered a round in his rifle. I was getting that Spiderman tingling all over. Oh boy, I thought, here we go again!

The driver stepped on the gas pedal and the truck accelerated like a rocket. Within seconds we were back in view of the school. The security police talked back and forth with somebody on the radio and decided to take me home. That was the second time in one day I found myself down by that part of the fence and once more I was able to leave unscathed. Perhaps I was pressing my luck; I didn't want to go back down there a third time.

Later, I learned that a jeep on the perimeter road at Subic Bay Naval Station had been ambushed recently. Machine gun fire from just outside the fence line had raked the jeep pretty badly. Nobody survived. Maybe that's why it was so quiet on the ride home.

As the truck pulled in front of our house, I could see one of my sisters, Michelle, playing in the front yard. I could tell that she was a little confused momentarily to see this large police vehicle stopping in front of our house. Come to think of it, my sisters always looked a little confused. Of course, as soon as she saw me, she ran in the house as fast as she could, yelling, "Mom! Dad! John's in trouble again!"

Everybody who was home came running out to investigate as I lowered myself down from the truck. Hanging my head down just a bit, I reached out for my mom and dad. It was good to be home. Of course I started crying again, but at least I was not shaking as much anymore. My family could tell something bad had happened to me. We all went inside to hear the story. It was kind of nice to hear things like, "What happened to you my poor son?" instead of the normal, "What did you do this time?"

As the two security policemen were talking with my parents, everybody else was quietly listening; everybody except David, my little brother. Being so little, he was being crowded out from the circle around the security policemen. So David did what any normal little brother would do in a similar situation. He positioned himself next to me and started tugging on my arm for attention, all the while whispering, "What happened? What Happened? What Happened?" over and over again.

Finally, I turned, and rather impatiently blurted out to him, "Dave, me and this guy were robbed and they still have him!"

Well, that shut David up all right. In fact, it shut everybody up. The next thing I know, everyone had stopped talking and they were all staring at me. It was a little uncomfortable to say the least. Quickly, one of the security policemen asked, "What do you mean they still have him?"

"My friend didn't get away, only I did," I replied. Goodness, I thought, hasn't anybody been listening to me?

Boy, did that set things in motion. Apparently, this whole time, nobody except me knew that Jim had been kidnapped. It finally dawned on me – as well as all of the adults in the room – that, although people had been listening to me, they just couldn't understand a word I was saying. Whenever I had tried to talk earlier, all I really did was cry. I could just hear what was going through the security policemen's minds: We've just wasted over 30 minutes!

The Dogs

For the third time that day, I found myself back in that same spot along the perimeter road. It wasn't long before other vehicles arrived on the scene. I have to admit, it was exciting. Several armed men were milling about the crime scene, some of them with military patrol dogs. A sense of urgency was in the air. There was some hope, however small, that we'd be able to locate Jim nearby, but already an hour or more had passed since I last saw Jim. With each passing moment, that hope was fading.

Some soldiers were walking into and out of the jungle trail left behind from my desperate escape. Overhead, a helicopter appeared, hovered briefly, and banked away to investigate things from above. A group of dogs were brought up to the edge of the perimeter fence and released. The dogs dashed across the fallen fence and started sniffing everything in sight, scurrying in and out of the jungle at a frantic pace. One dog still had a muzzle on.

I learned that the muzzled dog was not like the other patrol dogs; that one was an attack dog. Unlike patrol dogs, attack dogs received additional training above and beyond that required for normal patrol duty. Patrol dogs were trained to patrol, seek out, and defend themselves and their human partner from danger. Attack dogs were trained specifically for combat duty in Vietnam and as such these dogs were not very well suited for routine patrol duty. Because of the sheer size of Clark Air Force Base's K-9 training facility, it was not unusual to find a few attack dogs still around.

Running from a patrol dog was not one of the smartest things to do. Once a patrol dog caught up with its victim, the dog was trained to detain the person until his partner arrived. Running away only agitated the dogs and tended to make them forget their training. Occasionally, patrol dogs would chew on a forearm just to get their point across. On the other hand, attack dogs had a tendency to kill anybody they caught, regardless of whether or not they were surrendering. To an attack dog, everybody except their partner was fair game. That's why, outside of a combat zone, you almost always saw attack dogs muzzled. I could just imagine Jim being saved by an attack dog, only to be summarily executed by the carnivorous canine. What rotten luck that would be; not to mention embarrassing for the base commander.

It was against some local treaty for the security police to travel off base with their weapons – not that any of them wanted to – which is probably why the dogs were released to search on their own. There was a feeling that anybody bold enough to kidnap an American in broad daylight would not hesitate to shoot at or kill other Americans, even armed ones.

For now, there was nothing else to be done. A helicopter was searching overhead, dogs were beating the bush for trails, and a security police team was standing by waiting for an armed Filipino security escort to arrive. Not until then could a ground search be extended beyond the base's perimeter, but nobody knew exactly when that was going to happen.

A decision was made to try and notify Jim's parents. There was just one major problem: I had no idea what Jim's last name was. I didn't even know where he lived exactly, only that he lived down at the barns. So with that bit of information we set off to locate the parents of some red-headed kid named Jim, about 11 or 12 years old, who lived in a barn near the base's parade field. As we drove off in the truck, I glanced back on the scene behind me. Things were not looking good for Jim. I was beginning to think we'd never see him again, at least not alive.

The drive down to the parade field was a long one that day. Nobody said a word. I just sat there between the same two security policemen I had met earlier. I was mulling over several questions in my head: How would we find Jim's house? What if he didn't live at the barns at all? What if Jim, if that was his real name, was making the whole thing up? What if he didn't even live on base?

As it turned out, I shouldn't have worried so much. As we turned onto the first road alongside the parade field, there was Jim!

"There he is," I shouted. "That's him!" Jim was alive!

Wait a minute, I thought. He was alive, all right, but that meant he wasn't back in the jungle and he appeared to be okay. In fact, it looked like he was playing a game of ball with some friends. This was not looking good at all, I thought to myself. Suddenly my story was beginning to look like a big lie.

The security policemen stopped their truck in front of what was presumably Jim's front yard. He froze when he saw me in the truck. By the time the security policemen had approached Jim, he was crying. Whew, I thought. What a relief. This really did happen.

It turns out he really was kidnapped. Even worse, I had been chased. Jim explained what happened after Pete grabbed him. After I ran into the jungle, the two men I ran past chased after me while Jim was quickly taken across the perimeter fence into the jungle. There, Pete, Jim and the other two bad guys waited.

Shortly after, the two men who were chasing me returned. Jim said all five men began to argue, but he wasn't sure what was happening since he couldn't understand a word they were saying. Apparently though, the five men came to some sort of understanding. They took Jim's shirt and shoes, along with his watch and a necklace he was wearing...and then they left. Jim said he stood there for a minute, petrified with fear; almost too scared to even breathe. Then he ran all the way home.

The Hero

The security policemen told me that if I had been caught, Jim and I might not be alive. I may have in fact saved both of our lives by escaping. Now, all of a sudden, I was a hero. Of course, after the initial euphoria of the moment went away, I had some explaining to do. Like why was I down there in the first place? Besides that nagging circumstance, my claim as the hero who saved the day was generally accepted both at home and at school. However, after a few days or so, my heroics were promptly forgotten.

Jim, on the other hand, had some real explaining to do. He was in big trouble with his parents for even being near the perimeter fence in the first place. Turns out, he had been warned that trading across the fence was prohibited. Not only that, once Jim got home, he forgot to tell anyone what had happened. He was afraid he would get in trouble if he had done so. Never mind that I could have been kidnapped, or even killed, and nobody would have known. Jim was a bum

As for Pete and his merry band of kidnappers – nothing. Nobody in the nearby villages had even heard of a Pete. No big surprise there; Pete was probably not his real name anyway.

A year later, I was playing ball with a group of kids in the Grissom school yard and I saw Pete again. He was down at the fence. I was older and a lot smarter and even though some time had passed, I knew it was him all right. There were no breaks in the fence this time. Pete didn't seem to recognize me, but I recognized him right away. For a brief moment, I thought about running for the security police, but I knew nobody would believe my story if I told them. Besides, Pete would be long gone before I got back.

Some of the kids were talking to Pete, and he laughed as they talked. It brought back bad memories for me to see him again. I finally summoned up enough courage to talk to Pete. I asked if he had any weapons on him, to which he replied "no". Nonchalantly, I picked up a rock and contemplated throwing it at him. I wanted desperately to nail him right in the head. For some reason, I didn't throw the rock. Probably would have missed anyway, or started some kind of war or something like that. I wonder what ever happened to old Pete.

CHAPTER 4

Boy Scouts

I was blessed by God with the opportunity to be in the Philippines at precisely the right time in history and at precisely the right age to be a part of a grand adventure called scouting. If I had to name the one thing I liked best about my time over there, it would be the Boy Scouts. The Boy Scouts of America in the Philippines. What a concept. What an adventure.

Becoming a Boy Scout fulfilled a lifelong dream. My two older brothers, Tony and Mark, were scouts. Tony, my oldest brother, reached the rank of Eagle Scout, a remarkable achievement. And Mark, by all accounts, was a first class scout himself, although rumor has it he never reached that rank officially.

As a kid I remember my dad and me dropping Tony off at a campsite in Germany. The tents, the campfires, and all that camping stuff was just so cool. I remember a scout swinging a bucket, half filled with water, around and around above his head. Amazingly, no water fell out. For years, I thought that was a trick only Boy Scouts knew.

And everybody had pocket knives. Nobody seemed to mind, either. Heck, Boy Scouts were licensed to carry knives. The license came in the form of a Tote-n-Chip. If you had one, then by Boy Scout law – which some say is equivalent to federal law – you were deemed worthy to use a knife and a hatchet...provided of course, your Tote-n-Chip card had all four corners. Any small infraction or misuse with your knife would result in a corner to be cut off the card. Once all four corners were gone, you lost the privilege to carry a knife. Tony's Tote-n-Chip card was always in mint condition. On the other hand, Mark's card always looked more like a stop sign instead of a rectangle. Nonetheless, watching and listening to my two older brothers gave me inspiration to become a Boy Scout.

I can't remember the day I actually became a scout or how it happened; it just happened. The next thing I knew I was part of Troop 336, the Super Troop. I believed there was nothing we couldn't accomplish once we set our minds to it. Although today I think a more literal translation would be: some of us believed there was nothing we weren't allowed to do. To the casual observer, Troop 336 was more like a troop of wild baboons gone berserk.

Jungle Summer Camp

Once, I went to a Boy Scout summer camp for a week or so down near Subic Bay Naval Station. As a patrol leader, I had to go down a few days earlier to receive some additional training and to help scope out a campsite for our troop. The camp area we were using was being borrowed from the United States Marine Corps, who used the area as a training facility.

About 12 of us, along with two or three adult scout leaders, loaded our gear and ourselves into two trucks. These were huge two-and-a-half-ton trucks with green canvas covers on the back. With a couple of Marines as drivers, we took off from our pick-up point at Subic Bay and headed on down a jungle road for camp.

After driving for what seemed like miles, we stopped at a clearing surrounded by a thick, green jungle. The clearing was intended to be used as a common area for group activities like bonfires, contests, and standing at attention for the raising and lowering of the flag each day. Except for a small, white barracks near one end of the clearing, there was nothing else remarkable about the field. It looked like any other normal field of dirt surrounded by a lush, green jungle. The clearing was just newly expanded in anticipation of our arrival, courtesy of the Marine Corps. It really was a beautiful sight to see. Then it started to rain.

Rain

The sun disappeared. By the time we had unloaded the truck and put our stuff in the barracks, it was really coming down. Within minutes the parade field had become a field of mud. It was raining so hard you could no longer see the edge of the jungle from the barracks. The two Marines who drove us in suggested we start preparing ourselves for the night. Since there was no electrical power available, time was of the essence. Once it got dark outside, it would really get dark inside the barracks.

I claimed a wood-framed, army-issued cot over by one of the corners. It had a moldy, musty smell to it. Every military cot I ever slept on had that smell. At least the cot was dry and it sure was nice to be in out of the rain. I started unpacking. Even though it was still pretty early in the afternoon, I was ready for bed; it had already been a long day. However, the Marines advised us not to unpack our stuff just yet. Even more disconcerting was they told us not to make any plans to sleep on the cots either. They pointed out that it was raining very hard, and although the barracks floor was elevated two to three feet above the ground, there was a possibility the water level would reach inside. That, I thought, had to be a joke.

I immediately suspected a conspiracy by the adults to create fear and panic among the younger ranks. The scoutmasters were always trying to pull practical jokes on us, like sending the tenderfoots out on a snipe hunt, or to go find a left-handed hammer.

But we were not tenderfoots; we were seasoned veterans, at least in the scouting sense. We were all patrol leaders of some kind and to some degree we had all mastered the practical joke.

The Marines assured us the rain was no joke. We weren't in any real danger, they said, but it was possible we might get real wet. They explained that these types of rains will cause minor flooding and we should start taking the necessary precautions now. I reluctantly played along, but still maintained my claim on the cot over in the corner.

Parachute Hammocks

There was just one large room inside the barracks with a couple of closets along the walls and a few picnic tables. We positioned the tables in the middle of the room, then piled all our gear on top of the them. Inside the closets were parachutes. When it rained, the Marines explained, it was better to sleep in the parachutes instead of on the cots. I had to see this to believe it.

The Marines showed us how to make hammocks with the parachutes. We tied the ends of them from the rafters to form a neat row of hammocks running along the length of the ceiling. This was cool. The parachutes, we were told, were kept here just for this purpose. I was beginning to think this was a lot of work for a practical joke, but if we could really sleep in a parachute hammock suspended from the ceiling then I would certainly play along.

Any doubts about practical jokes soon vanished when water started to seep through the door and spill onto the floor. Time to get in the hammock. By the time it got real dark, the cots were submerged in muddy brown water. Soon, the water was lapping at the picnic table tops…and it was still raining.

We lay there in our hammocks while it rained. It was quite an experience, almost like we were sailors inside an eighteenth century British man-of-war, sailing off to some far away land in search of an adventure. You could hear the wood creaking and squeaking as we swayed to and fro. We even had rats!

Rats

Rats had taken refuge in the rafters as well. You could hear them scurrying about. It was spooky. We could see them with our flashlights. One thing was for sure, these were ugly rats.

When spotlighted with flashlight beams, they would drop down into the water and swim away. I never knew they could swim, but when the lights were out, the rats would always sneak back up into the rafters. Our imaginations got the better of us, because it seemed they were whispering to each other about who to attack first. We were afraid they were going to chew our hammocks loose. Fortunately, I think the rats were more terrified of us than we were of them.

Eventually the rain stopped and it wasn't long before we ran out of night-time stories to tell. We watched a few flashlights fall into the water and listened to a few people who just had to go to the bathroom. Finally, we all went to sleep. Except for the rats that is. I think they scurried about all night long.

Muck Field

The next morning, we woke up to find the water gone - all of it. As quickly as it had come, the water had gone away. Left behind was a thin layer of sediment on the floor. A high water line mark could be seen on the inside and outside walls of the barracks as well on the trucks. The ground around the barracks was now a field of mud. Although the sun would shine most every day for the next week and a half, that field never dried out completely. The sun would try its best to dry things out by day, but every night the humidity from the surrounding jungle would saturate the field all over again. Our parade field became known as Muck Field. It was because of Muck Field that I would become the muddiest and dirtiest I had ever been. Nonetheless, camping there became one of the best trips of my life.

At first, the mud and humidity bothered me; it bothered me a lot. Everything was either too wet from the humidity or too dirty from the mud. If you exerted yourself at all, you would immediately become soaked in sweat. There was always a risk of becoming dehydrated, a dangerous condition that could kill you if you were not careful. Generally though, dehydration would just ruin an otherwise perfectly good camping trip.

Once everything you owned got wet and muddy you forgot what being dry and clean meant. Only then could you start enjoying yourself. So, by the end of the second day, I started to enjoy myself.

Jungle Campsite

We soon found a camping spot big enough for our troop contingent. Located right off the far end of Muck Field, on the opposite side from the barracks, we picked a spot that appeared to meet our needs. Unfortunately, we had a lot of work to do; it was far from being a place to set up tents just yet.

The site we chose was about 20 to 25 feet off of Muck Field. Although the area was densely packed with vegetation, it was by and large free of any big trees. So over the next two days we slashed and hacked out a campsite. Eventually it took the shape of a lop-sided circle. We set up about a dozen two-man wall tents around the perimeter, each one facing inward. With the addition of two large picnic tables in the center, we had a textbook campsite. In some ways, it was even better. The canopy of the surrounding jungle created a cozy environment. Standing right outside the tents, it was difficult to see the sky, and from Muck Field it was impossible to see our campsite. It was like being on an expedition deep within some unexplored territory.

The Marine Corps gave us wooden pallets to put inside our tents. That was nice. The pallets gave us the opportunity to at least pretend we were dry, because even though the sun was out most every day following that initial rain, the canopy never seemed to stop dripping on us. Worse, as the week wore on, our campsite became just as muddy as Muck Field.

The tents we used were classic Vietnam-era, Army-issued wall tents. Big, green and roomy, the box shaped tents could comfortably sleep two people. There was enough floor space for two cots and camping gear. More importantly, the sides of the tent were high enough to allow us enough room inside to set up our mosquito nets. It was already bad enough trying to sleep in the heat and humidity each night; without our mosquito nets, it would have been unbearable.

Mosquito Nets

The Army issued a mosquito net kit which came with a large green net and two t-shaped metal stands. The stands were placed in the ground at both ends of the cot with the net draped over them. Cloth ties secured the nets in place. This formed a mosquito-proof enclosure over the entire cot, at least in theory anyway. Inevitably, one or two mosquitoes always got through. Every night the annoying high pitched whine of a mosquito could be heard as it zeroed in for a kill. The otherwise tranquil nights spent lying there listening to jungle sounds were always interrupted by the occasional slap of somebody missing another mosquito.

Eventually though, the campsite was complete. The rest of our troop arrived and the scouting began. A lot of activities were planned throughout the week. Things like first aid classes, knot tying, basket weaving, tug-of-war, and other events. These activities were scheduled to help us earn merit badges and to have fun. They were also designed to keep us busy and out of trouble. Unfortunately, the damp weather, some poor logistical planning, and the sorry condition of Muck Field forced the cancellation of many planned activities. That was a blessing in disguise, sort of. Once an activity was postponed or canceled, we were often released to entertain ourselves. It was always nice to have time to explore and play around, but having free time with the skills and tools to enjoy that free time is even better.

Rifling Merit Badge

It was here, at this summer camp, that I learned three of the greatest things in my life: how to make fire using only bamboo and a knife, how to make snares for catching wild animals, and finally, how to field strip, load and fire an M-16 rifle. With my new-found knowledge and time on my hands, I was no longer the simple Boy Scout from before. I was now a force to be reckoned with. Heck, I was downright dangerous; especially to myself.

As a Boy Scout, earning your rifling merit badge is one of the coolest things you can do. I mean, where else can you shoot a gun for free? For me it was particularly special because I had never fired one before, at least not a real one. One day, a small group of us loaded up into a truck and headed off for the firing range. I was beside myself with anticipation.

Somewhere nearby the summer camp lay the Subic Bay firing range. I was in awe when I saw the place. Rows and rows of firing stands could be seen up and down the range; each had a line of fire facing into the sides of large, jungle-covered hills. The place was practically empty when we arrived. Except for some Marines a few hundred feet away from us, there was nobody around.

As we unloaded from the truck, a crescendo of gunfire erupted from where the Marines stood. The hill downrange from their position was instantly transformed into a cloud of dirt and mud from impacting bullets. I was impressed. As quickly as it had begun, it ended as a "cease fire" order could be heard over a loudspeaker. We stood there transfixed. We had just witnessed the greatest display of fire power any of us could have ever imagined.

The Marine

We were snapped back into the real world by a loud voice from some big Marine standing nearby. It sounded like he was barking at us. We quickly fell into a line. We listened quietly as he yelled at us about how lucky we were to be alive on this fine day, not to mention the fact that before us lay some of the finest weapons the United States of America has ever produced. We just stood there and stared at him.

As he spoke, the Marine keep pointing at a table with several M-16 rifles lying on top of it. Apparently, the rifles were for our use. To top it all off, there were enough for everyone. My jaw dropped...we were going to get our rifling merit badge using M-16 rifles? It seemed unbelievable, but in a way, I guess it made sense. In order to earn the rifling merit badge, you needed to shoot a rifle. And these, as I thanked my lucky stars, were the only rifles available.

It seemed like forever before we could actually touch them. The rules seemed endless for what we were not allowed to do: no horseplay, no pointing the rifle in any directions other than downrange, no talking, no touching the rifles until directed to do so, and absolutely no horseplay. Okay already, I thought. Nobody is going to goof around. When do we actually get to fire one? We watched the Marine take the weapon apart and put it back together several times, then it was our turn.

It was something else to be holding an actual M-16 rifle. In a way, it was exhilarating, even though that first touch was not what I expected. It seemed almost like I was holding a toy. It was lighter than anticipated and was surprisingly easy to take apart and put together again, which was good since we had to demonstrate we could do that; not just once, but three times…each time having to pass a mini-inspection! This was beginning to seem like work.

Once we passed our inspections, we were instructed to lay our weapons down. Then the Marine walked down the firing line and gave each of us one round of ammunition. This, I believe, was the first time I ever held a live round. Boy, what a big disappointment! The M-16 round was incredibly tiny, at least when compared to most of the old bullets and shells I had been collecting. That's it? I thought, we only get one bullet?

We watched the instructor demonstrate the correct way to chamber a round and assume a proper firing stance. At a command of "fire at will," he shot at a target downrange. We all looked at each other with big grins, whispering things like "bullseye" and "I can do better than that." The Marine let us know, quite emphatically I might add, that the first idiot who shouts "where's Will?" in response to the "fire at will" command would have to eat their bullet.

Well, the big moment finally came. I loaded my rifle, took careful aim downrange and waited for the command to fire. I imagined a wall of enemy soldiers were charging my position and I was the only one who could stop them. Over the loudspeaker came the "ready on the left" and "ready on the right" commands. The tension in the air was thick. This was it.

The "fire" command and accompanying gunfire scared me to death. I almost missed hearing the command to fire altogether, as the crack of the guns on either side of me startled me into firing with my eyes closed. Just like that, it was over. I missed it.

The Marine congratulated us for earning the rifling merit badge. What a fine display of marksmanship, he said. I was just a little disappointed at how this whole thing had turned out, especially since I probably didn't even hit the hill behind the target. Heck, if this had been a real battle, we'd have been overrun.

Moving Target

Then a surprising thing happened...the Marine started handing out entire clips of ammunition! Each one of us received a clip with several rounds! Now we'd learn how to fire on automatic, he said. This didn't seem like the same jarhead who'd been yelling at us all morning; this guy seemed much friendlier.

This was more like it, I thought. We loaded and took aim for the second time that day. When the "fire" command came, I was ready. What I wasn't ready for was the cardboard cutout of an enemy soldier that popped up downrange out of nowhere. None of us were. Not only that, but the target was mobile...it was moving. As it moved rapidly from one side of the range to the other, it looked almost like an enemy soldier running across a field. The target swayed back and forth along its track as it made its way across.

The Marine and the voice over the loudspeaker became hysterical. They were yelling at us to shoot "him" before he reached the other side. Immediately, everybody on the firing line brought their weapons to bear on the target, or at least in the general direction of it. There must've been ten of us on the firing line, but I doubt more than one or two bullets actually strayed onto the target. But it sure looked impressive – almost like a staged movie scene where the hero outruns the machine gun bullets on his way to blow up a bunker.

Now that was fun. Most surprising to me about the episode was that I learned the M-16 rifle was not a rifle at all...it was a machine gun. Chuck Connors, the Rifle Man, fired a rifle; I fired a machine gun. After picking up all of our empty shells, we left the firing range. I never made it back there. Later in the week we shot arrows at the archery range. It wasn't quite the same.

Tents in the Jungle

Camping out for a whole week is always fun, no matter

where you do it, but camping out for a whole week in a jungle is an adventure all by itself. It was a challenge to keep the inside of the tents dry and clean and, at times, even to keep them standing. Pounding a stake into the wet jungle floor was a lot like burying it in the sand. Tent stakes were constantly slipping and had to be repositioned and guylines would become slack from moisture. The tents were perpetually sagging for one reason or another, and heaven forbid anybody would touch the inside walls of their tents.

A seemingly innocent act, tracing your finger along the inside of your tent was akin to turning a shower spigot on right over your cot. Why it did that was always a mystery to us at the time. Unfortunately, that never did stop anybody from doing that to someone else's tent. Today, I suspect that touching the inside of a tent has something to do with the disruption of the water's cohesiveness on the outer surfaces of the fabric; either that or it's an unexplainable form of water torture. There's nothing more irritating than trying to sleep on a hot, humid night with a mosquito in your ear and a constant drip, drip, drip of water somewhere on your body.

Despite the water torture and mosquitoes, we all survived intact. Camping like that was both a fun and a character building experience and I walked away from that trip with a great appreciation of the jungle...and the animals in it.

Mudfish

The jungle was alive with animals. In the mornings, we would wake to find wild boar tracks running right through our camp. As far as I know, none of us ever saw any wild boars, but I did manage to make a plaster of Paris mold of a boar track before heading back home.

One of the most interesting animals I ever came across was the mudfish. I'm not sure if these fish were really called that or not, but that's what we called them. They were indeed fish, and believe it or not, we found them buried in the mud. They apparently would become stranded once floodwaters receded and over time, the fish had adapted to this situation. It would flood often enough that all a stranded mudfish had to do was bury itself deep enough and wait until it flooded again. Provided the ground didn't dry out, the fish would survive.

I remember the first time I heard of mudfish. One day we saw a Filipino digging a hole in the middle of Muck Field. He said he was digging for fish; mudfish to be exact. We didn't believe him, but continued to pester him with questions. We asked why he was digging for fish in the mud, to which he replied, "mudfish are easier to catch in the mud". Besides, he said, they were good to eat. None of us took the mud fisherman too seriously, since he didn't have any mudfish with him. He left without finding one.

The next day we found one in the hole the mud fisherman had left behind. I guess he didn't dig deep enough. Overnight the mudfish probably thought all that commotion above was another flood. Whatever the reason, we found this big, slimy brown fish flopping around in the middle of Muck Field. It looked a lot like a muddy catfish from the Mississippi River. As you might guess, the news spread like wildfire…the great mudfish hunt was on.

Everyone, it seemed, was determined to find a mudfish. I never found my own, but I did find a lot of mud. There must've been some trick to finding the right spot to start digging. After a while, I stopped looking altogether; I couldn't stand to eat fish in the first place. Consequently, digging around in the mud to catch a fish seemed silly. Perhaps if I would've caught one I wouldn't have thought of it as such a silly endeavor.

A few people actually did find some mudfish. That evening, the smell of cooked mudfish hung in the air. It smelled like burnt dirt. Not only that, the meat didn't look much different than the mud it was found in. It even tasted like mud. By nightfall, mudfish mania had run its course.

Fruit Bats

During the day you could hear and see a great many birds chattering and flying about. I wish I would've spent more time looking at them. But there was one animal in the sky I was always on the lookout for: the fruit bat.

Fruit bats are huge. In fact, they are the largest of all the bats, with a wing span up to six feet. Unlike most other bats, fruit bats hang out in trees, not caves. If you looked hard enough you could see dozens, if not hundreds, of them hanging from the trees. Bats hanging from trees in broad daylight was quite a sight.

The first time I saw them in flight was at dusk. The sky was beginning to darken as the sun slowly disappeared beyond the hills. Several dozens of them were moving across the sky. Unlike other bats, fruit bats look extremely graceful in flight; their flight paths are amazingly straight and level. They appeared to be moving in slow motion as their large wings flapped up and down. At first I thought I was looking at large birds. When I learned they were bats, I couldn't take my eyes off them until it got completely dark. It seemed like there were hundreds of them in the sky. I'll never forget that scene.

Wild Monkeys

As interesting as the fish, birds, wild pigs, and bats were, there was no other animal as mysterious as the monkeys. Wild jungle monkeys. Small and very shy, these little guys traveled around in small groups and generally stayed away from the campsites. Unlike the monkeys in the Tarzan movies, it was difficult to hear or even see them at all. At least during the day.

They appeared to be most active at night. One morning we awoke to find our trash strewn all over the camp. Dozens of little muddy monkey footprints were all over the picnic tables. It appeared that sometime during the night they very quietly ransacked our trash, presumably in search of something to eat. The prospect of having wild jungle monkeys dropping in for a visit was just too exciting to pass up, so we did what any other self-respecting Boy Scout troop would do: we laid out some food and set a trap.

Now imagine our disappointment when no monkeys showed up that night, especially after just about everybody tried desperately to stay awake for the big event. To add insult to injury, by morning our picnic tables were covered with ants that were feasting on the food we left out for the monkeys. Great, I thought. We set a monkey trap and all we catch are ants.

The next night wasn't any better. This time, instead of everyone trying to stay up, we posted a rotation of guards to keep watch. In the morning, we awoke to find no food, a snare still set, and a whole roster of guards who slept through the night. There were a lot more ants, though. This was beginning to get embarrassing. We'd been robbed twice and stood up once by a bunch of dumb monkeys that nobody had ever seen. It was possible, we thought, that maybe they were not so dumb. Either that, or the monkeys and ants were working together to steal our food and make us look bad. Perhaps it was time to rethink our strategy.

The monkeys were obviously very clever, or just very shy. Our tents were arranged in a circle, all facing inward. In the center were two picnic tables. It was possible they were watching us at night. Unless everyone was asleep, or at least looked like it, they wouldn't come down from the jungle canopy. So we set more snares and forbade any talking whatsoever. All communications would be done through flashlights. An elaborate flashlight on-off language was developed to help us "talk" better throughout the night. This time most everybody took an afternoon nap to help them stay awake longer. We even filtered our flashlights through a sock to help cut down on the beam intensity, but as nighttime fell and everybody retired to their tents, the flashlight codes were quickly forgotten. After an hour or so, most everybody was asleep. I, too, fell asleep, but it wasn't a sound sleep. I found myself drifting in and out of my dreams so often that I lost track of time.

First Sighting

Somewhere in one of those moments where it's hard to tell if you're dreaming or not, I saw a monkey on the picnic table. They were here! I was suddenly wide awake, my heart racing. I had to restrain myself from moving as I lay there staring out through my mosquito netting. No more than a foot to a foot-and-a-half tall, he was kind of half-sitting, half-standing on the picnic table. He wasn't moving much, but he was definitely checking the place out. I looked for my flashlight only to find it was out of position. I wanted to alert the others about the monkey's presence but I didn't want to take any chances that reaching for the flashlight would scare him away, so I lay there and watched. (I later learned I was not alone in observing the arrival of the first monkey.) The stillness of the moment is something I'll never forget. It was the middle of the night, yet a soft glow illuminated everything outside. A heavy mist hung in the air. The jungle canopy cast a soft shadow down upon the campsite while the shadows created by the tents further enhanced our concealment by cloaking us in darkness. It dawned on me as I lay there that turning the flashlight on would've been a dumb move. As it was, we could probably see the monkeys better than they could see us. As long as we kept quiet, did not move, and kept our flashlights off, we could watch them all night long.

Another monkey dropped down from above, followed shortly by another. How many were up there? I wondered. I couldn't see any up in the trees, but there were probably more than the three I could see on the table. Two monkeys started scavenging while one tended to stay put most of the time. They looked like little wild jungle people walking and hopping around on the tables. One even made it all the way down on the ground. They moved about so effortlessly and stayed remarkably quiet...that is, until a snare went off.

The Snare

I had forgotten about the snares. The snare startled everybody when it went off, especially the monkeys. The triggering of it, followed by the instantaneous whooshing sound of the rope whipping through the air was immediately accompanied by all three monkeys bolting up into the canopy above. Unfortunately for one of them, it had indeed been snared. Ironically, we had captured the lookout. The snared monkey was yanked back toward the campsite, while the other two, along with the dozen or so others in the trees which I hadn't seen until they started moving – startled by the sound of the snare – scattered into the night. The monkeys moved at breakneck speed. Quite unlike their arrival, their departure was far from stealthy. From the moment the snare went off, the monkeys were screaming. The jungle was alive with noise; it was incredibly loud. Needless to say, everybody was awake. (Later I found out the entire summer camp was awake wondering what in the world was going on.) People stumbled out of their tents in disbelief. I, for one, couldn't believe one of our plans actually worked! But the real question remained: what do we do next? I don't think anybody ever considered that we might actually catch a real monkey. We did indeed snare one, but he was far from immobilized. Having been standing directly in the snare when it triggered, the rope tightened securely around his waist...but this monkey could still move.

A discussion about the snare is probably in order at this point. I saw people making them for the first time on this trip, a skill I would continue to practice whenever I got a chance during my stay in the Philippines. The whole concept behind setting a snare was so frontiersman-like that no self-respecting Boy Scout would pass up the opportunity. What impressed me most about the snares was how simple they were to make, but what really caught my attention was how powerful you could make them. Find a long enough, strong enough tree, and you could snare a man. The only requirement was the tree had to be flexible enough to bend, and stay bent, without breaking or snapping in half.

Finding the right tree in the right place was perhaps the hardest part, but even that wasn't too hard in the jungle. It was quite common to find 10- to 15-foot-high trees all over the place. Heck, you couldn't help but run into them. Trees grew like weeds in the jungle. The next hardest part was setting the trigger. Once you mastered that, you had it made. Every snare and trap I ever set had the same basic trigger, one I learned by watching one of our scoutmasters do it. He learned it while attending the Jungle Survival School at Clark. The trigger is such a simple mechanism that the school's instructors probably copied it out of Daniel Boone's diary.

Anyway, once you had chosen your tree and assembled the trigger, all that remained was to set the trap. Setting it was always my limitation. Young kids cannot set powerful traps by themselves; it's one of the basic laws of physics. In order to set a big snare, you need to be strong enough to actually bend the tree down.

The monkey snares we set in our campsite were set in place with a lot of teamwork. The trees we used were tall (a good 15 feet high), skinny, and grew just outside of the campsite clearing. We would bend them down, some of them arching right over a tent, and set the trigger mechanism directly to the picnic tables.

So when the snare was triggered, our monkey found himself dangling from a 10-foot rope tied securely to a 15-foot tree growing just outside our campsite. But unlike a pig or a rabbit, monkeys can do more than just dangle. To an animal that can climb, jump, and run better than any other animal in the jungle, ten feet of freedom in all directions is a lot of space.

And our monkey was mad. After realizing he couldn't escape by running away, he turned around and became downright belligerent. Spotlighted by half a dozen flashlights, the monkey, still screaming, leapt repeatedly in our direction, apparently in an attempt to attack us. I was startled to learn that monkeys had canine-looking teeth. Although this one didn't look like it stood any taller than a foot and a half, it still looked big enough to hurt someone.

Monkey Escape

I felt like an idiot. We just stood there gawking like a bunch of dummies at this magnificent creature we so carelessly captured. What were we going to do?

In time, the monkey was able to work free of the snare. All that running around, combined with some gnawing at the rope, eventually weakened the rope enough for him to escape. And just like that, it was quiet again. The whole affair couldn't have lasted longer than five to 10 minutes from the time I first saw the monkey on the picnic table.

Everybody was awake and milling around, talking about our wild kingdom encounter. Left behind was the mess the monkeys had made in their dash to get away, a chewed-up snare, and the fear that a war party of angry monkeys would return while we slept to avenge the humiliation of their lookout. Needless to say, nobody was allowed to set any more monkey snares; although, it's remarkable how our wild boar snares looked a lot like monkey snares.

Eventually our camping trip came to an end. That was the longest I'd ever camped out – almost a week and a half, and I believe it was the first time I had ever camped out in a real jungle. It wouldn't be the last time. For now, anyway, it was time to head home. On one hand, it was sad to leave behind our campsite, but on the other hand it was definitely about time.

All of us were filthy with dirt. Nobody had clean clothes or dry shoes, and all of us were just a little tired, both physically and with each other. Everybody went home in one piece, although we did have one minor casualty.

One guy cut his thumb pretty badly with a hatchet while chopping wood. A friend and I carried him on a stretcher all the way to the aid station. He probably could have walked but it made us feel important to carry him out of the jungle, across Muck Field and into the aid station using the stretcher. By the time we reached the aid station, we had attracted a small army of inquisitive gawkers wondering what had happened. We hung around and waited while our wounded compatriot was stitched up and bandaged. For a moment there, my friend and I thought perhaps we would get a Boy Scout Medal of Honor or something. Instead, all three of us got a lecture on how to use a hatched properly while our buddy's Tote-n-Chip was unceremoniously cut in half. Once the aid station personnel found out we were the infamous monkey-snaring patrol, we suffered even further humiliation by means of a veiled accusation that we were probably not chopping fire wood in the first place. At least not for a fire, they said. More likely, they suggested, we were fashioning punji sticks for a wild boar trap. Now there was an idea, I thought. To top it all off, we had to drag that stretcher all the way back to camp. At least it wasn't so heavy this time. Nonetheless, the jungle summer camp was a trip to remember, but it was by no means the best.

CHAPTER 5

Crow Valley

Our troop went on countless camping trips and hikes. We camped in places named Bataan, Camp O'Donnell, and Corregidor, and although they'd never let us camp at Crow Valley, I always wanted to. Crow Valley was a real valley. Ringed by mountains, it was used as a target and bombing range for military fighter and attack-bomber aircraft. On some nights, you could hear the man-made thunder rolling through those hills. I don't think I had as much a desire to camp there as I did just to see the place. I always wanted to know what it would be like to take off and go screaming through there at 500 knots. I never made it to Crow Valley.

City in the Sky

I did, however, camp at Baguio City. Not just once, but twice. Baguio City was beautiful. Located at a much higher elevation than most cities in the Philippines, people referred to Baguio as the "City in the Sky." There were so many low-hanging clouds it looked as if they were drifting all around us, with some dragging right along the ground in front of us.

Located atop a mountain, the landscape of Baguio was transcendental in nature. There were even pine trees. And if that in itself wasn't unusual enough for a tropical island, the air always seemed so crisp and cool; it was even rumored to have snowed there on occasion. It seemed incredible to me that smack in the middle of a land overrun with hot, humid jungles, there existed such a place. Yet there it was; winding mountain roads, tall trees, and no elephant grass anywhere. It was a pleasure to camp there.

Camp O'Donnell

Another memorable campsite was at Camp O'Donnell. I'm not sure what military significance that place had from 1972 to 1975, but it did serve in part as a small recreation facility for U.S. military personnel stationed in the Philippines. It had the added benefit of not being very far from Clark. Camping there would've been boring except for one thing: the lake. Well, it was a pond really, but we liked to think of it as a lake.

There were a couple of canoes we could paddle around in and a small floating pier from which we could fish. The pond was stocked with some weird tropical version of a Texas Bluegill, but it was still fishing. Moving to the Philippines from the Back Bay of Biloxi, where fishing and crabbing was almost a daily event, had left me with withdrawals. It was nice to fish again, even though my line would always get hung up on the weeds. The warm water and ever present tropical sun produced a constantly expanding mass of weeds in the lake. They looked like the type of plants you would buy in a pet store for a tropical fish tank, only the Camp O'Donnell weeds were bigger. And longer.

Swimming in the lake inevitably led to an encounter with the slimy clump of weeds. That, combined with the presence of venomous snakes in the area, always put a damper on things. Swimming in weeds was dangerous, because if you got tangled and panicked, you could drown. I wasn't too worried about drowning though; instead, my problem lay in the fact that my imagination couldn't distinguish a weed from a snake. So much for the swimming. However, the snakes were cool to watch, from a distance anyway.

There was one thing very special about Camp O'Donnell; something I'll talk more about later, but mention briefly here. Camp O'Donnell was a prisoner-of-war camp during World War II. Some say it was more of a death camp than anything else. Many Americans and Filipinos died there; yet there I was, only 30 years later, fishing.

Beagles and Pirates

The camaraderie I shared through the Boy Scouts was priceless. Friends with names like Bill, Tom, Mark, Stan and Don are forever burned into my memory - other American kids like me, serving time along with their families in a faraway land.

Our Boy Scout troop formed patrols with more traditional names like Bear, Deer, and Eagle patrols, but to me the best were the Beagle and Pirate Patrols. The Beagle Patrol's mascot was Charles Schultz's famous dog, Snoopy. That was the first patrol I ever remember belonging to. Our patrol patch even had a picture of Snoopy on it, which was kind of cute. Actually, that was the problem: it was too cute. It wasn't long before the Beagle Patrol mutated into the Pirate Patrol; the one I remember best. A friend and I created the Pirate Patrol from scratch. I was its first patrol leader.

Ever since I saw the Boy Scout patrol flag my older brother Tony designed and made years ago in Germany, I had always wanted to do the same. His flag had a dark green background with a Mickey Mouse character on it. My flag was red and black with a skull and crossbones emblazoned on it, complete with a dagger in one eye. I even designed a patch to go along with it. One of my scoutmasters used to say that flag was the black flag of the troop. He commented once that if he didn't know any better, he'd swear we were born and raised on a pirate ship. All flattery aside, our scoutmasters were a great bunch of people. I learned a lot from them.

Scoutmasters

We were lucky to have the scoutmasters we did. They came from all walks of the military: medical technicians, security policemen, and pilots...we even had one who was a wing commander. It was hard to keep the scoutmasters around for very long though; people were constantly rotating in and out of the base. It wasn't uncommon for some to arrive and be reassigned after being on base for only a year. Plus, there was a war on in Vietnam. Some of the pilots I knew would be leading a scout meeting on Wednesday night and on Saturday they would be flying a sortie across the Mekong Delta.

One assistant scoutmaster we had, a K-9 handler, was especially well-liked by the troop. One night while on patrol, he came across two Filipino nationals breaking into an airplane parked on the flight line. The perpetrators started running and our scoutmaster's dog badly mauled one of the robbers. We never saw that scoutmaster again. We heard that he and his dog were on the next plane out of the Philippines. Though his actions were justified in the line of duty, once he injured a Filipino national, he became subject to the laws of the host nation, which, unfortunately for some, weren't the same as those in America. A timely trial wasn't guaranteed and sometimes how good your prison accommodations were depended in large part on how much money your family had. Disputes between Filipinos and Americans, if not dealt with carefully, could easily strain relations between the two governments, no matter who was at fault or how minor the offense. The best way to handle our K-9 scoutmaster's situation was to remove him and his dog from the Philippines as quickly as possible. Or so I was told.

Speaking about crime and punishment, I once heard about the time somebody hopped in a brand-spanking new fire truck and drove it off the base. This was no ordinary emergency vehicle; it was a flight line fire truck designed to extinguish dangerous aircraft fires. Shortly after it arrived on the base, somebody walked up, hopped in, and started it up. With the sirens blaring and lights flashing, the fire truck sped across the flight line and onto the road leading to Friendship gate. Of course, all of the cars yielded the right-of-way to let it pass. Unfortunately, the security policeman at the gate let it pass on through as well; they thought the fire truck was on its way to put out a fire. By the time everybody figured out what had happened, it was long gone. But how can anybody hide a fire truck, especially one like that? Well, it turns out, not very well. The vehicle was soon located by the proper off-base authorities, but unfortunately the proper off-base authorities didn't want to give the fire truck back...at least not for free. If the Americans wanted it back, then all they had to do was pay the recovery fee, which I understand was pretty substantial. In fact, the recovery fee was so exorbitant, it was cheaper for the Air Force to have another one delivered from the States. I have no idea what ever happened to the stolen fire truck, or if this story is even true; but what the heck, it sounds interesting.

Dad the Scout Leader

The best assistant scoutmaster I ever remember was my dad. I don't think he was ever officially designated as an assistant, but he helped out enough that he might as well have been the scoutmaster. I liked having him along on campouts and hikes, just because he was my dad; other kids liked having him along, not only because he was a very patient man, but because he was fun. Dad had a knack for making us laugh.

Once, during a hike, we stopped to rest under a tree alongside the road. It was a hot day as usual. As the patrol rested, dad quickly dozed off into a nap; he was famous for falling asleep quickly. Dad's naps were never very long, because after only a few minutes he'd wake himself up with a loud snore. However, this time dad didn't have to wait for a snore to wake him up – he was covered with ants.

Ant Attack

Dad looked like an ant farm. Instead of panicking, he calmly, but very quickly, took most his clothes off. He brushed the ants off himself and shook them out of his clothes. At first we were all concerned, but it soon became apparent that he was going to be okay. Then everybody starting laughing. I'm sure a lot of the laughter had to do with the fact it was the middle of the day and we were next to a road and he didn't have any pants on, but instead of getting mad, he made the best of the situation and laughed about it. I mean, how many "ants in the pants" jokes can one person take without ever losing his cool? Especially on such a hot day.

Coconuts

Another time, Dad was showing the Pirate Patrol how to crack open a coconut. We all had one, but none of us knew how to open them, which by the way is not easy. After watching us flail away on the coconuts for a while, Dad called us all together into a circle. He explained how the proper tools are essential for doing the job right; not just for opening coconuts, but for any job. Dad was always good at seizing just the right moment to teach us something. Usually it had something to do with safety – his big thing was safety.

Dad picked up a coconut and held it in his hands. As he slowly turned it over, he spoke to us about concentration. It was a "focus your thoughts on the coconut and you cannot fail" type of message. We sat there, our eyes transfixed upon the coconut as Dad said to think of it as a crushable object. Then with his eyes closed, he started chanting: "Coconuuut, Jooohn's head. Coconuuut, Jooohn's head." Before anybody could start laughing, Dad let out a loud "AAEEEIIIII-YA!" and smashed the coconut to the ground. It cracked open. We were awestruck…and we had lots of coconut to eat that day. As for me, I had to endure sporadic chants of "Coconuuut, Jooohn's head" followed by the thud of a coconut hitting a rock for close to a month or so.

The Bamboo Table and RED HORSE

Two topics couldn't be more unrelated to each other than the bamboo table and RED HORSE. The only thing in common between the two was an event: a table decorating contest.

Our scoutmaster inadvertently entered our troop in the competition because he mistakenly thought it was a table building contest. Troop 336 prided ourselves on our rope lashing ability and rightly so since knot tying was a big part of any get-together we had. Whether it was playing a game to see who could tie knots the fastest or building a 50-foot long monkey bridge, our troop was good with ropes. Naturally, our scoutmaster thought a table building contest would be right up our alley and we agreed. So we set out to build a picnic table out of bamboo.

We made it a point to construct our table entirely out of natural materials; not one nail or screw was used. We lashed pieces of bamboo together using rope and strands of elephant grass. We even took it one step further and made all the table settings. We fashioned forks, spoons, knives, cups, bowls and plates out of bamboo, accompanied with woven place mats made out of elephant grass and a large bamboo pressure cooker for rice. We were confident we would win the contest.

Imagine our surprise when we showed up to find a bunch of old ladies hosting an elegant table decorating contest. How embarrassing. What's worse, our scoutmaster made us take turns standing by our table while everybody walked by to view the entries. It was downright humiliating. Luckily, I stood my watch pretty early in the day before it got real crowded. After that, I was released until the awards ceremony that afternoon.

To kill time, me and a few other scouts left the building and wandered around outside. It was another hot day and things were quickly shaping up to be a boring afternoon...that is, until we stumbled upon something most unusual. Parked behind one of the nearby buildings was a vast array of heavy construction equipment. Huge tractors, scrapers, and bulldozers – all painted dark green and bearing the distinctive RED HORSE emblem. RED HORSE; I'd heard of these guys. They were the Air Force version of the Navy Seabees. If you needed an airstrip quick, RED HORSE would get the job done, even under combat conditions. (By the way, it wasn't until I was in the Air Force years later that I learned RED HORSE stands for Rapid Engineer Deployable Heavy Operational Repair Squadron.)

Before us stood a magnificent display of heavy machinery. Just looking at the machines gave me an urge to build something. As luck would have it, the area was unattended and unguarded. That left us with only one option: we quickly scrambled onto the equipment.

It was almost as if we had found a sandbox with giant

playground toys. This sure beat the table decorating contest. We shouted commands back and forth as we imagined ourselves driving the machines over hills, through the jungle, and even buildings. We turned steering wheels, stomped on pedals, and pulled on levers as we played. One guy even managed to start one of the scrapers up – talk about instant fear!

The loud, unmistakable roar of a diesel engine, especially when you're not expecting it, is enough to scare the pants off of any kid. Everybody stopped playing as all eyes turned to the scraper. A puff of black smoke shot out of a pipe extending skyward above the scraper's cabin. The kid inside was petrified with fear. We all were.

Almost on cue, we all scrambled down and started yelling at the kid to turn it off, jump out, and anything else we could think of that made sense. Of course, none of us even knew how to drive a car, let alone a several-ton scraper. Fortunately, the kid did manage to shut the machine off. We ran back to the table decorating contest, just in time to see our table win First Place in the "Most Unusual" category. Those old ladies probably made that category up because they felt sorry for us.

Jungle Survival Training: Day One

The Clark Air Force Base Jungle Survival School was designed as an outdoor classroom to teach pilots, navigators, and other air crewmen how to survive and evade capture in enemy-held jungle terrain. The school's campus was cleverly designed to pack as much of a jungle-like atmosphere into as compact a space as possible. To be effective, the campus needed to be realistic, right down to the plants and animals. Cages of every size and shape were integrated into the landscaping, with enclosures cleverly designed to hold snakes, wild pigs, alligators, birds, and more. The bird cages were especially cavernous in size. One cage in particular was enormous; it housed a couple of the largest raptors in the world: the monkey-eating eagle. Only the harpy eagles of South America matched the sheer size of the Philippine monkey-eating eagles. As the name implies, these predators would hunt, kill, and eat monkeys. Armed with massive talons, the eagles would feast on primates snagged right out of trees. I never saw one in the wild, although I often dreamed that I would someday.

I saw some film footage once of a harpy eagle snatching a monkey out of a tree. Diving in undetected, the impact from the aerial assault was enough to kill its prey instantaneously. As the eagle flew away, the monkey just dangled in its claws. From a distance, it appeared as if the giant bird was carting off a dead man to feed its young. Even more frightening was footage of the same eagle attacking and carrying off a very large sloth. This time the photographer was able to record the eagle as it brought its prey to the nest. Because of its relatively large size, the sloth was able to survive the eagle's aerial assault. The unfortunate mammal was alive when it reached the nest – and awake. The bird held the sloth down with its large talons as it started to feed her young chick. As one might suspect, it was disturbing to watch as the sloth struggled to regain its freedom, but to no avail. Like the harpy eagles of South America, the Philippine monkey-eating eagles were dangerous jungle predators and our scoutmasters often warned us that the littler scouts in the troop were always in danger of being snatched away by one. I'm not sure everyone believed that story, but it did help reinforce the "buddy system" of traveling in pairs – just in case. I did, however, get to see the two monkey-eating eagles held captive at the Jungle Survival School before they were released or moved to Subic Bay. I felt sad for them; as big as their cage was, it wasn't big enough.

One of our scoutmasters arranged for us to take a watered down, three-day version of the survival course right before the school closed down for good. I even saw Charlie, the famous chicken-eating snake. The first day we spent watching the instructors set snares, make a fire using only a knife and bamboo, make a hat out of banana leaves and other neat stuff. One of the neatest things I learned was how to get water from the water tree. The water tree had massive above ground roots buttressed against its thick trunk. The roots would gradually taper downwards and fan out across the jungle floor. The tree's thick, heavy vines, like everything else in the jungle, would continually grow and before long become hopelessly entangled with the surrounding canopy. Although the tree was very solid and stout, it was a virtual sponge when it came to holding water. All one had to do was locate one of its vines and cut a small segment off. Held level, it looked like any other vine one might expect to find in the jungle, but when tipped to one side, pure clean water would drip, drip, drip out. By cutting a one-foot section and tying a rope at both ends for use as a shoulder sling, one had an instant canteen. In the tropics where the heat and lack of clean drinking water could lead to heatstroke in the blink of an eye, the water tree was a miracle.

Jungle Survival Training: Day Two

On the morning of the second day we learned about evasion, which reminded me a lot of playing hide-and-seek. Later that afternoon we hopped on a truck to a real-life jungle outside the base somewhere. The place we arrived at was used as a training range. The truck dropped us off by a helicopter landing pad and we were each given a parachute, a knife, a canteen with water, and a military issue survival kit. The kit contained matches, a signaling mirror, a candy bar, iodine tablets for water, a small sewing kit, and a small amount of first aid supplies, along with some other assorted stuff. Just getting the kit was worth the trip.

We were to pretend we had just been shot down over enemy territory and our job was to survive, evade capture and be rescued. Actually, all we had to do was wander around for the rest of the afternoon, find a place to sleep, and meet back at the helicopter pad in the morning. To make it more interesting, we'd be "hunted." Employed by the school as trackers, Negritos would begin searching for us at first light the next morning. We were considered "captured" if they found us before we reached the helicopter pad.

The rules were pretty simple: split up and hide as best you could, don't wander across the mountains, and don't get hurt. I had grand plans on how to evade capture but once the truck left, the only thing I could think about was not losing sight of anyone. I was beginning to dread the loneliness of the situation. Well, it wasn't that bad or dramatic. After all, there were eight to ten of us on the trip, plus one adult who knew how to do this for real. It was just a little humbling to be in what seemed to be the remotest place on the face of the earth.

Aside from the occasional sound of an aircraft engine overhead, there was no other indication of human life outside our immediate vicinity. And the stories we heard didn't make matters any better...our scoutmaster told us about lost Japanese soldiers who still roamed these very jungles. Great, I thought. With my luck, it was only a matter of time before I stumbled upon a Japanese patrol who still believed we were at war.

Well, you can imagine how the day went. We couldn't make any fires (silly thing to do when you are trying to hide) and we had to be very, very quiet. No talking, unless absolutely necessary, was the rule. Nature, on the other hand, had a way of bringing the loudest whispers out of the best of us, especially when somebody unexpectedly came across a big spider or bug. We did manage to find a couple of magic water trees, which was good since everybody was running low on water...and food. After only an hour into the exercise, nobody had any survival candy bars left. Soon, everybody was hungry. Of course, nobody was starving enough to eat any bugs yet, but we all managed to get our fill by eating the insides of a couple of banana plants, the heart of which contains a long and tender shoot about as tasty as a raw stick of celery. It was nonetheless juicy.

Nightfall

As nightfall began, it became evident that nobody was going to split up and bed down alone, at least not willingly. With a little coaxing from our scoutmaster, we did manage to spread out a bit. By the time I actually found a spot to sleep, I couldn't see anybody else around, mainly because it was already dark outside. I'm sure I wasn't the only one that was scared, but I didn't want to be the first person to break the no talking rule. Just in case though, I was standing by to yell as soon as I heard anybody else.

My spot was going to be up in a big tree. I carefully checked to make sure I left no telltale signs behind: tracks, pieces of paper, anything the enemy could use to find me. Drenching myself with insect repellent, I climbed up the tree and wrapped myself in the parachute as best I could, so tired that not even my fear of snakes, lost Japanese patrols, or falling from the tree could keep me from sleeping.

Jungle Survival Training: Day Three

I awoke the next morning almost exactly in the same position I fell asleep in – crooked. I slowly began to regain my senses. Somewhat alarmed at first, I was surprised to find myself in a tree. It took me a few seconds to remember why.

It was very early in the morning, but already the jungle floor was covered with shadows from the sun as it filtered through the canopy from above. As time passed, I could see more and more rays of sunlight begin to cut through the darkness. I remember looking around, but not moving, partly because my body was aching and it would hurt too much to move and also because I couldn't see anybody else around, which frightened me a little. I was definitely alone. Slowly my fear was replaced by the urge to relieve myself. I was just about to stretch out a bit when…I saw him.

The Hunter

Moving through the jungle in the direction of the tree I was in, I could see a shadowy figure. It was a Negrito. At first my heart jumped, fearful of who it could be, but I soon recognized him as one of the Jungle Survival School guides. He was a "hunter", whose job it was to track me down. His gaze was fixed on the ground before him as he advanced. He was moving so slowly and cautiously that it almost seemed as if he wasn't moving at all. I wondered if I was hidden enough, but didn't dare move a muscle to find out. Any movement, I thought, would quickly reveal my position, so I lay there, in the most uncomfortable and increasingly agonizing position.

I watched the Negrito as he slowly found his way across the jungle floor. He passed right near my tree before disappearing from my field of view and just like that, he was gone. I didn't have enough courage to turn my head and see if he was truly gone, so I sat there a while longer, just to be sure. I strained to listen for any telltale signs of movement, but aside from the normal sounds one hears in the jungle, I couldn't distinguish anything out of the ordinary. Eventually, my desire to relieve myself became paramount. I carefully turned my head in the Negrito's last known direction. Nope, I couldn't see him. He walked right by me, I thought, feeling just a little proud of myself for hiding so well. As I sat up in the tree, any elation I might have been feeling over my stealthiness quickly vanished. There, at the base of my tree, stood the Negrito. Well, at least now I could relieve myself without worrying about how much noise I made.

The Negrito helped me gather up my things and led me to the rendezvous point. Good thing, I thought, since I really had no idea where the rendezvous point was. On the way there I tried to make conversation by asking him questions like, "How did you find me? and "Was it hard to find me" and stuff like that. His English was terrible and I had a hard time understanding him, but as near as I could tell, he didn't "track" me down nearly so much as he had "smelled" me out. Apparently, the bath I had given myself with insect repellent the night before was my downfall. It had been effective in keeping the bugs away, but it eventually betrayed my position. There was a lesson to be learned in there somewhere, but at the moment, I was too tired and sore to care about it. I had spent less than 36 hours in the jungle. Hardly enough time to justify a medal or anything, especially since I ended up being captured.

CHAPTER 6

The Greatest Camping Trip

I can't remember the actual date or even what part of the year it happened, but it did happen. It was only an overnight camping trip, yet in that brief time I experienced more fun than I ever had in my life. It truly was the best overnight camping trip I can remember. I'm sure the location had a lot to do with it, as is always the case, but this time it was extra special. We camped on the grounds of the Clark Air Force Base Jungle Survival School, or at least what was left of it.

After 1973 the American ground war in Vietnam was officially over. The Jungle Survival School at Clark Air Force Base was shut down and was consolidated with the school at Subic Bay. All the animals and anything else salvageable were shipped off. Left behind were a few buildings once used as classrooms and a bunch of animal cages. Also left behind was the man-made jungle surrounding the school. Designed to bring as wide a variety of flora and fauna together as possible in such a compact space, it was a landscaping wonder. The jungle literally flowed around the buildings and cages and trails were cut to connect different areas together. Cultivated for years, the campus grounds were nothing short of beautiful.

But now it lay empty. Gone were all of the snares and traps once used as instructional aids; anything that could've been moved had been and nobody remained behind to look after the place. It was deserted. Walking through the trails was like walking through the abandoned ruins of some lost, ancient city. It was the perfect place for a campout.

I'll probably never know how we ever got permission to camp there. The school had not been closed for very long before somebody along the line must've been given the job of finding out what use there was for an abandoned jungle survival school. If I had to guess, I'd say it was a former Boy Scout. He must've recognized the school as a potential camping site and an idea was born. As far as I know, we were the first Boy Scouts to camp out there. As things turned out, we were probably the last.

We arrived at the school sometime in the mid-morning. There were perhaps 20 scouts along on this trip and as best as I can remember, only one scoutmaster. After a brief period spent unloading and locating a place to pitch our tents, a good friend of mine named Bill and I took off. It was cool. We explored as many trails as we could find. I say that because as nighttime fell we were still finding new ones, which was remarkable, considering the school grounds were not all that big. But the most interesting part, at least initially, were the cages.

Some of the cages were comparable to those one would find at a large stateside zoo. Some had big, heavy steel bars set into concrete while others, particularly the big bird cages, were nothing more than giant screened enclosures with doors. Nonetheless, all of them were open. Technically they weren't open, only unlocked. And according to the Pirate Patrol's interpretation of the Code of Ethics for the Boy Scouts of America on the Philippine Island of Luzon, that meant the cages were open and free for use. For that matter, we later discovered, all the buildings were open too! It was fun exploring the cages.

Capture the Flag

The cages came in handy during our traditional capture the flag game. We used them to house our prisoners. It sure was a lot better than the make-believe prisons we were normally stuck with. Now if that's all that had happened that night, it would've been a great night to remember. For you see, capture the flag is about the best game I've ever played in my life. Playing it under those conditions only made it better. I can't explain how challenging and thrilling it is sneaking around, charging enemy positions, running away from the enemy, taking prisoners and capturing the flag. I feel sorry for the poor guy who never got to play that game as a kid.

The Discovery

Earlier in the day while exploring one of the trails, I came across something interesting. Actually, as I was running alongside a trail, my foot hit something. I knew right away that whatever I bumped into was probably special. Stopping, I went back and bent down to see what it might be. Whatever it was, I needed to feel around for it a bit since the ground was covered with grass. I finally found it, and as suspected, it wasn't a rock. It was a small piece of rusted metal...my heart began to race.

Finding a piece of rusted metal just off of a trail in the Philippines usually only meant one thing – something from the war. Frantically clearing the remaining grasses away, I could see that only a small portion was showing of what appeared to be a large object. I couldn't budge it at all. I tried kicking it to loosen it up, but that didn't work. So, I started digging. First with my fingers and then with a small stick. Slowly, the object became more and more distinguishable, and then, suddenly, I recognized what it was. I had stumbled upon a bomb. And from all indications, it was a big one. Without hesitating another moment, I ran away as fast as I could.

The Bomb

Looking back through the years, I wish I could say that I was running away to save myself from blowing up and to warn everybody about the potential danger in our midst; but no, I was running to tell Bill about what I considered to be the greatest archeological find of the century. The way I figured it, I needed to tell someone about the bomb for two reasons: first, it's no fun to find something cool if you can't share it with at least one person, and second, it looked way too big to dig out all by myself. I'd need help.

Bill and I returned to the bomb site and began digging. Trying to be as inconspicuous as possible, we eventually dug it all the way out. We made a pact not to tell anybody else about the bomb, especially our scoutmaster. We didn't want to share our discovery with anyone, least of all have somebody take it away. Once we had it completely dug out, we sat back and examined our prize. It was the biggest bomb I'd ever seen; it was at least three feet long and extremely heavy. Neither Bill nor I could lift it for very long by ourselves. It was so heavy in fact that it required the both of us to actually move it anywhere, which presented us with a dilemma: what good was it? We could hardly move it, which obviously meant we couldn't drag it home without somebody noticing, but we couldn't just leave it there for somebody else to find either. So we came up with a brilliant idea: we re-buried it. We decided to wait until it got dark and then come back and get it later. Of course, it would have to be much later since Bill and I had already developed an elaborate plan for adventure that evening; one that even something as exciting as a new-found bomb couldn't derail.

The Plan

Eventually nightfall did arrive. We ate dinner, built our traditional bonfire, and started playing capture the flag. Located in a more remote part of the base, the Jungle Survival School grounds were surrounded by fields of tall grass, ideal for capture the flag. Normally, we'd play capture the flag all night long. That was good, because as soon as we started the second game, Bill and I put the plan into action. We formed up with our team and told them of our daring plan to sneak into the enemy's camp and steal their flag. All we needed was a diversion. While our team created one on the far side of the field, Bill and I slipped undetected into the enemy's territory, which was remarkably surprising considering how hard it normally was to do that without getting captured. Even more surprising was doing it without being seen; and the game had only just begun! By and large that would have been a very good set of circumstances. In this case, it was very bad.

Bill and I wanted to get captured. Unbeknownst to even our own teammates, the plan was to get caught as early as possible. That way, we would have to sit the game out until the next one started. Once detained, nobody cared about you. Most of the time, prisoners just went over to watch the campfire. Nobody cared what they did as long as they stayed out of the game. A good game of capture the flag would last anywhere from 45 minutes to an hour. Getting captured early would have given Bill and me plenty of time to do what we really wanted to do without anyone noticing; that was the plan – only it wasn't working.

Instead, here we were not five minutes in, standing right in front of the enemy flag, and not a soul was in sight. The opposing team didn't even post any guards. All Bill and I had to do was grab the flag and race across the field back to our territory. We'd be heroes. Unfortunately, getting captured was the plan; winning the game was not. Bill and I didn't have all night to do what we really wanted to do and time was slipping away. What we really wanted to do was go visit a place a few miles across the field; a place we knew was off limits. Yet a place so steeped in mystery and lore that going there became our quest…we wanted to raid the Airplane Graveyard.

Airplane Graveyard Raid

The Airplane Graveyard. It was a place where a lot of airplanes returning from Vietnam went to die. Planes ended up there due to a lack of spare parts or battle damage. Once an aircraft arrived in the graveyard it was cannibalized for parts. During the day we could see the tails of some of the planes far off in the distance. We had heard about the place from one of our scoutmasters and ever since Bill and I wanted to go there. Badly.

Standing there before the enemy flag, we came up with another brilliant plan: Plan B. It was a good thing, too. Bill and I forgot the prisoners were being locked up in the vacant animal cages. What a waste of time that would have been. Of course, a better plan would have been to win the game and start a new one. Anyway, Plan B was an okay plan, which was to hide the enemy's flag. Actually, we just threw the flag as far into the field beyond the enemy's camp as we could. We figured the game would last longer since neither side knew where the flag was hidden. Not only would our own team be unable to find the flag, but neither would the enemy. The game could conceivably last for hours. That would give us more time to raid the graveyard. With the enemy's flag properly disposed of and armed with flashlights, Bill and I took off.

It took a lot longer than I thought, but we eventually reached the outskirts of the graveyard. The area was not as well-lit as it probably should have been. In fact, it wasn't illuminated very well at all; it was actually very dark in and around the planes. Far off in the distance, I could still see our campfire. Even further beyond the graveyard in the opposite direction of our camp, I could see the bright lights from the flight line illuminating the sky and somewhere out past there lay the perimeter. It was kind of spooky.

There were several different types of planes scattered about the yard. I, for one, was in awe of the number and size of the aircraft. All of them were big. I could recognize several of the planes, most notably the McDonnell-Douglas F-4 Phantom and Republic F-105 Thunderchief. Unfortunately, we couldn't get into any of the planes. They were apparently locked. More likely though, I think Bill and I were too weak and stupid to figure out how to open them up. Trying to be as sneaky as possible, we crawled up onto several of the aircraft, but none of the cockpits were open. We must have looked like bumbling idiots.

After the initial thrill of actually making it all the way to the graveyard wore off, we rather reluctantly decided to start heading back to camp. We were just so disappointed we hadn't come across any souvenirs to take back. Without any proof, nobody would ever believe we sneaked over there. All that changed when we stumbled across an RB-66 with a fuselage hatch open. Working together, we managed to climb aboard. It was dark outside, but inside it was pitch black. We had to keep our flashlights on continuously. Up to this point we had only used them to peek into cockpits or into shadows. We knew the longer we kept our flashlights on, the greater our chances of being detected, but so far, the graveyard appeared to be completely deserted.

RB-66

The RB-66 was bigger inside than it looked from the outside. Built originally as a bomber, then converted into a reconnaissance aircraft, this particular plane appeared to have been modified for use as an electronic jamming aircraft. Technically, that would make it an EB-66. Of course this discussion isn't relevant to the story because at the time I thought everything bigger than an F-105 was a B-52. The RB-66 had several interior compartments in addition to the cockpit. It even had a little hallway of sorts. One console in particular drew my attention; it had a chair located in front of some type of radar screen. The radar had a little wall around it, shaped like the type of covering seen around the eyepiece of a submarine periscope. Apparently, the person sitting there would lean over and stare into the radar, presumably to look for missiles or something. The covering was almost certainly a shield of some sort meant to block outside light. It was obvious the plane had already been cannibalized for parts; aside from the radar, it was not all that interesting inside. It was pretty much picked clean.

We did manage to salvage an instrument or two from the cockpit dashboard. One of the components I removed looked like a horizon indicator. At least it was something. I had visions of finding a joystick, but there weren't any to be found. Heck, even the pilot and copilot chairs were gone. Bill and I decided to go, it was getting late. We walked back to the fuselage hatch and tossed our treasure down onto the ground. Just as we were about to jump down, a light flashed into our eyes, accompanied by a command to "FREEZE!" In the background I heard the low, growling sound of a dog. That did it. Now I was really scared.

Captured

Although we weren't instructed to do so, Bill and I immediately put our hands in the air. It seemed like the natural thing to do under the circumstances. After our hands went up, we froze in that position. How ironic; after all we went through earlier in the night, Bill and I were captured anyway.

Apparently the graveyard was not deserted after all. Before us stood a well-armed security policeman with his K-9 companion. Equipped with an M-16 rifle and a bright flashlight, he asked us questions and we answered. I learned long ago that getting caught doing something you know you're not supposed to be doing can only get worse by lying about it. (I learned that in Biloxi, Mississippi – but that's another story.)

First the security policeman wanted to know how we got out there. We told him. Then he wanted to know what we were doing. Bill and I told him, although I think he had figured that part out when we dropped our loot on the ground. Then he wanted to know what we intended to do with the stuff. We didn't have a very good answer, but we mumbled something anyway. Finally, he asked us what we thought he should do with us. For the life of me, I can't figure out why authority figures ask that question. Do they actually think the culprit will respond with, "Arrest me and take me home so I can get in even more trouble?" Neither Bill nor I answered that question, mainly because I didn't think, "Uh, how about we forget this ever happened and just let us go?" would go over too well.

Surprisingly enough, though, that's exactly what he did; he let us go. He even let us each keep one item as a souvenir! As near as I can tell, as soon as he saw that Bill and I weren't a real threat, he stopped being all serious and became friendly. He even let us pet his dog. Actually, he said we could touch his dog, but his dog never really stopped snarling at us, so we both passed on that one. The security policeman watched us throw the rest of the junk back up into the RB-66. When we were done, he walked with us toward our campsite. He seemed like a really nice guy. Looking back, he was probably only 19 or 20 years old. Heck, he was probably a Boy Scout himself only a few years earlier. Once we reached the edge of the graveyard, he told us to be careful and hurry straight back to camp. And with that, Bill and I turned and almost ran all the way.

Needless to say, we were amazed at our luck. I've often wondered if we just happened to stumble across the nicest security policeman in the world or if we were let go for some other reason. I suspect he let us go because he couldn't readily explain how two kids wandered into the graveyard, much less an airplane, undetected. He was probably sleeping.

We arrived back at camp to find everyone sitting around the campfire. Immediately Bill and I were implicated in the disappearance of the missing flag. We quickly shifted the focus of the conversation to our graveyard adventure. Of course, nobody believed us. But once we showed them the equipment, we became gods, especially in the eyes of the younger scouts. As we told the story over and over, it got better and better, until it grew into what it is today.

Back to the Bomb

Later, after some people turned in for the night, Bill and I went and retrieved our bomb. It never ceases to amaze me how difficult it is to find things in the dark. It took us a while, but we did manage to find it. Of course, it was right where we left it. This time, however, we came prepared – we brought some rope. Now, what happened next, I'm not particularly proud of. In fact, I'm reluctant to write any of it down, lest some poor idiot attempts to do what we did.

I don't know when exactly, but sometime that night, Bill and I hatched a plan to detonate the bomb. We tied the rope around the base and dragged it through the field to a tree. Throwing the other end of the rope over a tree limb, we hoisted it up into the air. Now, this rope, being a long rope, allowed Bill and I the opportunity to take some cover behind a nearby knoll. Secure in our belief that we were safely protected, we both took a deep breath and released the rope. The bomb fell and hit the ground. Nothing. Except for the thud of the impact, nothing happened. So we tried it again and again. We even stacked some rocks under it thinking that would help. It seemed our bomb was a dud. We must've lifted and dropped that thing a hundred times that night, but all we got was tired. A few stragglers from the campfire wandered over to watch us. You'd think there'd be at least one level-headed person in the group, but that was not the case. Nobody seemed overly concerned that it might explode. In fact, everybody was disappointed that it didn't. Eventually, people didn't even bother to hide behind the knoll as the bomb was dropped. It didn't take long before the bomb was abandoned all together. Everybody who was still awake was tired of playing with it by that point. The bomb was simply left under the tree for the rest of the night, it even had the rope still attached.

The few scouts still awake migrated back over to the campfire. There's nothing like staying up late on a camping trip just to sit around a fire. The sparks, the smoke, the sight of red hot coals – all had an intoxicating effect on us. There were always one or two people who'd just sit there like zombies and stare into the fire, speaking only occasionally. Others would remain quiet as they poked a stick or tossed wood into it. But at least one person was always talking – and the things we'd talk about! We'd spend hours chatting about most everything: adventures we had been on, adventures we wanted to go on, school, family, rocks, girls and so on. I wish now somebody would've recorded all of those discussions, but nobody ever did. Too bad.

The Flare

I can't remember exactly who saw it first. Not that it mattered much anyway, because before long we'd all seen it. Off in the distance, across the great elephant grass plain, a flare had been fired into the sky. It was a red one. As it drifted slowly across the sky, we all took turns trying to explain the relative importance of a red flare going up so late at night. None of us really knew what it meant, but we did come up with some pretty good explanations.

One person thought it meant the base was under attack; another said maybe it was a distress signal from an injured airman. There was even some discussion about what a green flare versus a red flare meant. Other flares began to appear in the sky. Then a faint popping sound could be heard in the distance and we could see what appeared to be tracers cutting through the distant darkness. Machine gun fire! Somebody was shooting at something.

At this point, we became sufficiently alarmed that we quickly extinguished the fire and woke everybody up as quickly as possible. The flares and the gunfire were obviously several miles away from us along some portion of the perimeter road. Huge fields of elephant grass with the occasional tree or bush separated us from the action. Although it was far away, it looked close. I remember our scoutmaster being concerned as he directed us to stay low and to stay together. We huddled just inside the jungle line of the survival school as we continued to watch the show. Some of the younger scouts were visibly frightened. Of course, the older scouts, like myself, were much too stupid to be scared. Someone even suggested we move in for a closer look. That idea was quickly nixed by our scoutmaster.

Counter-attack

A helicopter could be heard flying overhead somewhere, but none of us could see it in the dark. Before long, other helicopters could be heard. At one point, some people claimed they saw machine gun fire originating from a helicopter as it shot at targets on the ground. Soon, the shooting began to wane as fewer and fewer flares could be seen. Slowly I began to feel that whatever was happening was about over. Suddenly, we heard the loud rumble of engines moving behind us. Tanks!

Actually, they weren't tanks, but more like gigantic armored cars...and there were only two of them. Still, that was enough. Each vehicle had six huge wheels: three on each side. (Or was that four big wheels: two on each side?) Anyway, it seemed like the tanks came out of nowhere. Following behind were some jeeps loaded with heavily-armed security police. Both tanks stopped near our campsite and more people with guns got out of them. Without much delay, the soldiers fanned out and began to move forward into the field in the direction of the flares. The tanks slowly advanced along with the troops. The soldiers didn't seem to be in any particular hurry, but no time was wasted either. I could hear some soldiers barking commands in the dark while radio chatter from walkie-talkies filled the air. It was like we were in a war movie. As quickly as they had appeared, they were gone.

Two airmen stayed behind to watch over us. Of course we flocked around them as they came closer. We immediately bombarded them with questions ranging from, "What's going on" to "Are those real bullets in your gun?" It always took a while, but somebody would eventually ask, "Have you ever shot anybody?" The airmen seemed to enjoy the attention, but they never really turned their eyes from the direction of the shooting. Our scoutmaster asked a few serious questions, but it became obvious that nobody knew exactly what was happening. We were told it wasn't a training exercise, though, but if it wasn't that, then what was it?

Judging from the conversation between our scoutmaster and the airmen, plus the bits and pieces we heard from their walkie-talkies, either the base was attacked by communist guerrillas or somebody accidentally shot their M-16 at somebody else, thereby triggering a massive retaliatory response by the security forces. (The next morning the stories ranged from a "rebel excursion onto the base was successfully repelled" to "several wild pigs were killed as they inadvertently strayed across the base's perimeter.")

Regardless of what was happening, it appeared to be over. Eventually, boredom and fatigue got the better of us and we went to bed. When morning came, the airmen were gone. And that ended the greatest night of my life. In less than 24 hours I had found a bomb, played capture the flag, raided the airplane graveyard, and witnessed a possible attack on the base. Not to mention that we were camping in a man-made jungle loaded with empty cages and crisscrossed with trails.

Dad and the Bomb

The morning after a camping trip was usually anticlimactic. Scouts would struggle to get out of bed and once they did, then one by one, they would congregate near the remains of last night's campfire. Everybody was usually dressed in what they slept in, their faces and hands covered in dirt, and their hair sticking up in unnatural ways. Their clothes smelled like campfire smoke. People would moan and groan as they moved in what seemed like slow motion. This particular morning seemed worse than normal and given the events of the previous night, maybe it shouldn't have been all that unexpected. Still, if I didn't know any better, I'd say those tanks from the night before rolled right through our camp and wounded everybody.

Since this was only an overnighter, we started to break camp and clean up our mess. It always amazed me how quickly we could disassemble our camp, especially when it took so long to set it up. Within minutes, all the tents were down, backpacks were packed, and people began to police the area. To "police the area" meant to walk around and pick up all the junk and trash. We prided ourselves in leaving a camping spot better than we found it. Soon, all that remained of our campsite were the impressions of our tents in the grass. Even any evidence of a campfire was hard to find once we buried it. Just like that, it was over.

My dad arrived to bring me home. Standing there among the other parents and scouts, Dad asked me about my trip. I told him all about it. As I spoke, he stood there gently rubbing the top of my head with his hand, something he did frequently. I guess that was his way of letting me know he was still listening, even though he was probably thinking of something else. As I spoke, I became more and more excited about the events from the night before and began to talk faster and faster. It wasn't until I got to the part where "...and I found a bomb and we tried to explode it..." that I realized I may have said too much.

Dad's hand stopped rubbing and gripped the top of my head. He slowly turned my head up to face him. Looking into my eyes he asked, "What did you say?" Although he spoke calmly, Dad was no longer smiling and the fact that he stopped rubbing my head was a sure sign of danger. I ruled running away out as option since he had a pretty good grip on my skull, so I thought I had better answer him.

"I found a bomb and we tried to explode it?" By answering

meekly and carefully wording my response as a question, I somehow hoped to defuse a potentially explosive situation – a common tactic employed by children against their parents when confronted with imminent danger. Sad to say, it's a tactic with little documented effectiveness. But I did like the "we" part of my answer. It always seemed to lessen the blow if others could somehow be implicated.

Now I really didn't have much to fear from my father, at least in physical terms. My dad was a very loving and gentle man. I can only remember him raising his hand against me two times before in my life, which is absolutely amazing considering the number of opportunities I presented him. Not only that, but considering the circumstances of the other two events, one could hardly consider those spankings.

Floor Towels

Once, during a particularly heavy downpour, Dad asked me to help him outside. It was raining very hard. He and I had to dig a little ditch to redirect the flow of water as it poured down a small hill behind our house. I felt proud to be helping him with what seemed like so important a task. Standing out there in the rain digging that ditch, I imagined that together we were saving our home from a great flood. In reality, all I think we ended up doing was making our neighbor's yard a little soggier. Still, it made me feel good to help out.

Called in for dinner, Dad and I went inside to wash up. Standing over the sink in the bathroom, we talked as we washed our hands. Dad thanked me for helping him. After drying his hands, he handed me the towel so I could dry mine and as I was finishing up, he asked me to drop the towel on the floor. That was a strange thing to ask, I thought. I looked up at him, then back at the towel in my hands. I figured, what the heck…so, I dropped the towel. Then he slapped me.

It wasn't a hard slap by any measure; needless to say though, I was stunned. I held my hand up to my cheek and looked up at him. Dad said not to drop any more towels on the bathroom floor because Mom was getting tired of picking them all up. Then he rubbed my head and left. Still in a mild state of shock, I turned and followed him out. Weird, I thought, for Dad to do that, but as word got around, the number of dropped towels on the floor in the boys' bathroom went down significantly.

The second time Dad hit me was right after one of those family arguments where everybody was yelling about something. I remember it was a weekend, sometime during the day. Dad ended the argument by telling everybody to stop arguing and not raise their voices in anger. The next person who raised their voice would get a spanking. He stomped off outside and Mom started vacuuming while everyone else returned to their chores. I was working at the kitchen table when I noticed something I needed was not there. I knew my brother Mark had it so I called out to him. Unfortunately, I had to call out loud enough to be heard over the vacuum cleaner. I don't think Mark ever heard me, but Dad did. He stormed in, and true to his word, spanked me. Then he left.

I stood there slowly realizing what had just happened. I would have cried if the situation had not been so ridiculous. Still, I never saw Dad so mad.

The next morning Mom came to me and said Dad tossed and turned all night because of what happened. How strange, I thought, for Dad to do that. Up to that point, I had always thought of him as being invincible. When he got home from work that day, he apologized. I was beginning to learn that Dad was only a grown-up version of me.

Strangely enough, both of those episodes occurred in the Philippines. Before, while in Mississippi, I did some things that deserved spankings. Later, after we left the Philippines, I did several things that probably deserved much worse. Dad never spanked me, though. Weird.

Clobbering Time

After I told my dad about the bomb and what I tried to do with it, I found myself on the ground. Dad clobbered me. I didn't even see it coming, but man, I felt it. I don't think anybody else saw it coming either. We were standing in a group of people when he hit me, and immediately afterwards everybody stopped talking and stared blankly in our direction. Then he turned and went to find the scoutmaster, presumably to beat him up. I just lay there and cried, both from the pain and the embarrassment of the situation. Later, I cried because I was ashamed of how stupid I was to do that with the bomb. That was the third and last time I can remember my dad hitting me. Not surprisingly, Dad never apologized for that one.

The EOD unit was quickly dispatched to the scene. The bomb was indeed a dud. Thank goodness. If it had exploded, the grassy knoll we were hiding behind would have afforded little protection. It was well inside the kill zone of the bomb and, in fact, would have been a part of the crater from the resulting blast.

The ride home was quiet. When we got home my bullet collection was dumped into the nearest EOD amnesty box, including two Japanese fragmentation grenades which I thought I had properly defused. It didn't make things any better that Dad didn't even know I had them in the first place, let alone hidden up on a shelf in the house. To make matters worse, it turned out the fuses were still intact. Only years of rust and neglect had prevented them from exploding. Dad let me keep the Japanese helmet, canteen, old rusty rifle, and bayonets, but everything else had to go. Over time, I picked up a few bullets here and there, but never in the quantities I once did. And I never, ever touched anything again that even resembled a bomb. At least not until I got to Corregidor Island.

CHAPTER 7

The Library

Soon after we moved on base, school let out for the summer and I was immediately bored. I was still involved with swimming and scouting, but neither of those activities required much of my time. If television had been available, I would have probably wasted the rest of my waking hours watching cartoons.

One day Mom took me and some of the other younger kids to a library. I believe it was the one at Wurtsmith Elementary School, for grades first and second. I enjoyed going there. What a great idea to keep the school libraries open during the summer. Not only did it give us kids something to do, it eventually led to one of the greatest discoveries of my life.

Browsing the shelves, I came across a series of history books written for children. This particular series caught my attention for two reasons. First, it had more pictures than words, and second, it was about World War II. Thumbing through the pages of those history books had quite an effect on me. I saw tanks, airplanes, ships and soldiers from every major World War II combatant. I never realized World War II was so global. Buried in that series was one book in particular I'll never forget.

Bataan

On the cover were the words "Bataan" and "America's Greatest Defeat". I can't remember the exact title - only those words. Pictured beneath the title were a bunch of men standing in front of the entrance to a large tunnel. They had their hands raised in the air as if they were surrendering. The men looked tired and beaten. At first, I wasn't sure what to make of either the words or the picture, but as I skimmed through the pages of the book, I came upon a startling discovery: Americans had been beaten in battle. How could that be? I thought. How could the Americans, the good guys, ever lose a battle? I thought the Americans never lost, at least they never did on television or in the comic books. Sure, I knew some Americans were wounded or even killed in war, but to actually lose such a large battle seemed so inconceivable. Even more shocking was the revelation that Bataan was a place in the Philippines. An entire American army had been beaten in the Philippines!

I checked that book out and read it from cover to cover. It was probably the first non-fiction book I ever read completely. My curiosity led me to seek out and read other books about the war in the Philippines. I learned about places like Corregidor, Bataan, and Fort Drum. I learned about the great American retreat, the Fall of Corregidor, and the infamous Bataan Death March. It all began to make sense. I wondered how I could've been so stupid. I knew the bullets and bombs I was finding were from battles between the Americans and the Japanese, but I never stopped to seriously think about the circumstances surrounding the conflict.

From that point on, whenever I found a bullet on the ground, came across a cave or crawled over some kind of fortification, I couldn't help but stop and think about the people who fought and may have died there. I became a self-styled student of the war in the Philippines. I even did a book report on the subject when school started up again.

Gradually, by reading books and building airplane and tank models, my knowledge of World War II history grew. Surprisingly, I learned quite a bit by reading comic books like G.

I. Combat and Sergeant Rock. I'm by no means an expert on World War II, but I do know that between 1936 through 1945, the vast majority of the people on this planet suffered through a war of unimaginable proportions and terror. And here I was, thirty years later, picking up souvenirs.

Death March

You can imagine my surprise when I heard about our troop's upcoming fifty-mile hike. Our troop was planning a fifty-miler? Fifty miles! How could anybody walk that far? Even more amazing was the planned route: our troop was going to hike along the very same road as the Bataan Death March. As silly as it may sound, my first reaction was one of fear. How could we do that without dying?

To begin with, we weren't going to walk as far, as fast, or under the same conditions as the poor souls of the Bataan Death March. True, we'd be walking along the same road, but there were some major differences. The original march started near the tip of the Bataan Peninsula and ended some 88 miles away to the North at Camp O'Donnell. We marched in the opposite direction, starting 50 miles away from the tip of the Bataan Peninsula and finishing on a beach near Mariveles, a small coastal town on the peninsula.

Second, we used a standard military issued two-and-a-half-ton truck to haul all of our camping gear, including tents, backpacks and cooking utensils. Towed behind the truck was a "water buffalo" – the nickname for a 500-gallon water tank on wheels. The plan was to hike fifty miles in three days: twenty miles each the first two days and ten miles the last. The truck and water buffalo would drive ahead three miles, park, and wait for us to catch up. Once we caught up with the truck and water buffalo, we would be forced to take a rest. Believe me, nobody had to be forced to take a rest. Walking three miles in that heat and under that sun was difficult to do. It would get extremely hot. Once we reached the sea, we'd camp out on the beach. The next day we'd all pile in the truck and head back home.

The people on the real Bataan Death March were not so lucky. They were forced to march the entire way with very little water and food. Dysentery, malaria and other tropical diseases were rampant. Rests were infrequent and many stragglers were shot, stabbed and killed. The heat and sun were a murderous combination. Merely stumbling would bring unwanted attention from the guards, even death. It's a miracle anybody survived at all.

Things didn't improve much for the survivors once they reached Camp O'Donnell. The living conditions and treatment by the Japanese were only slightly better than on the road. For the Americans and Filipinos who surrendered to the Japanese, Camp O'Donnell was a piece of hell on earth.

Fifty Miler

Twice, I hiked the fifty-miler Death March route. I'm proud to say I made it all the way both times, although one time I almost wished I had stayed home.

I have learned that walking instead of driving is the best way to actually see things. Unlike traveling in a car, as you walk you can feel the ground beneath you. You can smell the air and hear sounds you'd never hear if you were driving. Sounds like dogs barking, trees rustling in the wind, or the grind of your boot as you marched along. There was plenty of time to look at things; time to stop and pick up a rock or stick to toss. Yes, walking had driving beat when it came to sightseeing, but walking under the blazing sun and stifling heat of the Philippines sure made me appreciate the comfort of an air conditioned car. Man, was it hot.

The road we marched along was not a particularly busy road at all, although by Filipino standards I think it was a major highway. It was a two-lane asphalt road with wide dirt shoulders on both sides – straight and level for the most part until the last ten miles or so. Then it became a hilly and winding road.

The first forty miles of our march took us through wide open countryside. Sugar cane fields and rice paddies could be seen for miles. Farmers tended their crops with carabao-powered plows. We'd march for a mile or more without seeing anybody and then suddenly we'd come across a little town or gathering of huts. People would come out and say hello and wave to us. Occasionally, a farmer would give us some sugar cane stalks to chew on as we walked. Chickens and dogs were everywhere it seemed, especially around the towns. The few cars that drove by would honk their horns as a greeting and the people in them would lean out and wave. Although there didn't seem to be a speed limit, nobody really drove all that fast...except for the Rabbit Buses.

Rabbit Buses

Rabbit Buses were a common sight along the roads in the Northern Philippines. Their speed was legendary. Red buses adorned with a little white rabbit on each side, Rabbit Buses were perhaps the cheapest and quickest way to get from point A to point B in the Philippines. Unfortunately, the drivers seemed to rely more on a good horn than a good set of brakes. It wasn't uncommon to read or hear about another Rabbit Bus plunging off a cliff somewhere, killing all the people, chickens and dogs on board. But man, you could sure hear them coming.

First you'd hear the low rumble of the engine roaring up on you, followed by a barrage of horn blasts. If you were quick enough, you'd have enough time to see the red blur of a bus zoom by, followed quickly by a cloud of dirt and exhaust. The passage of a Rabbit Bus always left everyone shaking their heads and wondering why anybody would ever risk their life to ride on one of those.

Even more ubiquitous than the Rabbit Bus was the jeepney (pronounced jeep-knee). Brightly colored and adorned with every type of hood ornament imaginable, they were nothing more than elaborately decorated jeeps with no brakes. Whereas the Rabbit Bus was more of an open road cargo carrier, the jeepney was a high speed inner city taxi. When it came to safety, they weren't much better than riding a skateboard off a cliff. Although it seemed impossible, I do believe more people could fit in a jeepney than a Rabbit Bus. Ask any jeepney driver how many people you could fit into one and he'd tell you: "One more."

Memorials

Perhaps the most sobering part of hiking the Death March route were the memorials we came across. There were never any signs along the road announcing their presence. There weren't even any indications on our maps that they even existed...they were just there. We'd come around a corner, or into a clearing, and just like that, there would be one.

Most were simple in design and construction, usually a cement post with a plaque. A few were quite elaborate. One in particular I remember was a very large white rectangular-looking stone box with intricate decorations carved into the sides. It looked like a huge coffin, which was fitting I suppose, since we were told that this memorial was a tomb. Inside were the remains of Americans and Filipinos who had died during the Death March. Denied a proper burial during the war, the remains of many of the soldiers were located and placed into the tomb after the liberation of the island. Unable to identify the bodies individually, they were placed collectively in the tomb. The passages of the memorials were usually marked with silence.

Fifty Miles in Three Days

As mentioned earlier, our strategy for completing the march was pretty simple. Hike twenty miles, stop and camp. Hike twenty more miles, camp again. Then finish up with a ten-mile hike and campout on one of the beaches of the Bataan Peninsula.

Once, after hiking twenty miles, we set up camp inside the grounds of an all-boys' school. As luck would have it, the school was also the home to a Filipino Boy Scout Troop. We camped out that night side-by-side with them. Unfortunately, we weren't in the mood to sit around a campfire or play any games with our hosts. Given the fact that we were very tired and sore, about all we were up for was to eat and go to bed. Capture the flag was out of the question. Besides, the language barrier between the two troops was a challenge all in itself. I'm not sure how the idea came about, but the next thing I knew, the other troop had decided to put on a show for us.

The Joke

The school grounds had an outdoor stage. We gathered around and watched in awe as the host troop performed. They sang songs, did dances, and put on a puppet show. I couldn't understand a word of the songs but the puppet show was in English and it was entertaining. When they were done, they invited us up on the stage, presumably to sing them a song. We just looked at each other in fear; we didn't know any songs, at least not any real ones. Besides we looked terrible compared to those guys. While the Filipino Scouts were immaculate in appearance, none of us had any uniforms that matched. We looked more like a scraggly band of pirates. I don't think any of us even had a complete uniform.

After some persuading by our scoutmaster, we got up and sang a couple of verses of "Ninety-Nine Bottles of Beer on the Wall" and the classic "Row, Row, Row Your Boat." As for the puppet show, we decided on a skit instead. Actually, it was more like telling a joke. Now, you have to remember the situation here. These were kids telling other kids a joke. It's not even a very funny one, but it's worth repeating because of what happened.

The joke starts out with five people on the stage. One guy was a Russian General and the other guys were generals from England, France, Italy and the United States. The Russian General starts the joke by boasting about how he can beat any other general's army in combat. The English General responds with, "Oh yeah? Well, I have 100 tanks and 100 planes!"

The Russian replies, "No problem. My troops will eat yours for breakfast!"

The French general says, "Oh yeah? Well, I have 200 planes and four battleships!"

The Russian general counters with, "No problem. My troops will eat yours for lunch!"

The Italian general declares, "Oh yeah, well I have 500 tanks, 500 planes and 50 battleships!"

Again the Russian boasts, "No problem. My troops will eat yours for dinner!" Turning to the American general, the Russian general asks, "And what about you, you American swine? What do you have?"

Calmly, the American says, "I have 100 miles of barbed wire."

Looking confused, the Russian general asks the American general what he hopes to accomplish with 100 miles of barbed wire. To which the American general says, "Not much. I'd just like to see your troops eat THAT!" ...at which point everybody is supposed to laugh. Except nobody laughed.

Apparently, we underestimated the extent of the language barrier, either that or our hosts didn't think our joke was funny. The entire Filipino contingent was just sitting there staring blankly at us, almost as if they were waiting for the punch line or something. Seconds went by like hours. Even our own troop was not laughing, probably because they didn't want to be associated with a bunch of losers.

I had to do something. I felt partially responsible for us flopping. After all, the joke was my idea. Not only that, I was playing the part of the American General. Thinking quickly, I decided to do something which to this day I have no idea why. I yelled out a loud "AAAHHHH!" and jumped on the Russian General. Almost as if on cue, the rest of the generals attacked each other in mock combat. All of us were yelling. Then something most unexpected happened: the audience erupted with laughter. After a few seconds of pretending to beat up on each other, we stopped. Unbelievably, we got a standing ovation. I'll never forget that episode for as long as I live. I just know there's a lesson to be learned in all that. I'm sure it'll come in handy someday, probably during a boring meeting or something.

Camping on the Beach

Eventually, we did reach our destination. Camping on the beach was quite unlike anything I'd ever done before. It was wonderful. Well, at least it was beautiful. True, the beaches were wide and clean, coconut trees were everywhere and the water was clear and inviting. Some of us had even brought our swimming suits, except nobody told us about the sharks: the waters were shark infested. From the beach you could occasionally see a dorsal fin cutting through the water and as a consequence I never saw anybody go swimming. Besides that glaring oversight, and except maybe for the aggravation of having sand in everything, including our food, the beach sure was a neat place to camp.

One nice thing about camping at the beach was the wind. At first, it was annoying because everything we tried to set up kept blowing away. Then, somebody discovered that by facing our pup tents towards the sea, the wind would keep the tents up. All you had to do was stake in the corners. The wind was strong and constant enough that the tent would inflate and stay that way. No poles or guy lines required. It was quite a sight to see. Little orange pup tents lined up and down the beach like balloons.

Nightfall came. The wind never stopped blowing, but we didn't care much. It was a nice change from the hot, stagnant air we were used to camping in. The gentle sound of the surf was nice, too. We spent a long time sitting around staring out to sea. I wondered if pirates were out there.

Shortly after nightfall, I could hear explosions. They weren't very loud – almost like distant thunder – coming from just beyond the surf. The older scouts said the fishermen were dynamite fishing. If we were lucky, they said, we might be able to find a fish or two on the beach, maybe even a shark! Of course everybody ran down to look for dead sharks.

Unfortunately, all we found were dead jellyfish and aerosol cans…lots of aerosol cans. Over the next hour or so we must've found a few hundred of them. The cans were not labeled but they were full of something. Where they came from was a bit of a mystery. One theory was a passing ship may have crashed or dumped them overboard for some reason. Being good scouts, we picked up as many as we could and threw them away.

The Bonfire

Earlier, one of the scoutmasters bought an old nipa hut from one of the nearby villages. It was in very bad shape. The roof had holes in it and some areas of the floor were completely rotted through. I couldn't believe he paid money for it. Still, it was a good-sized nipa hut and kind of cool to have in our camp.

Up on four stilts, the thatched roof must have reached at least ten feet off the ground. Word spread quickly that the nipa hut, or what was left of it, was going to be our bonfire. Throughout the rest of the day any piece of driftwood, clump of dried grass, or burnable trash we came across was stuffed into it. By the time we were ready to start the bonfire the nipa hut was completely stuffed with debris. Everybody gathered around to witness the lighting of the bonfire and soon the entire hut was ablaze. It was by far the biggest campfire I'd ever seen with the flames reaching as high as the tops of the coconut trees. The heat was intense. Then came a loud bang.

The first few bangs caught everybody off guard and soon the frequency increased rapidly. It was almost as if giant popcorn kernels were exploding in the fire. With each blast, burning fragments could be seen shooting through the air. The nipa hut was exploding and people scrambled for cover.

Soon, the banging stopped. Closer inspection of some of the smoldering fragments solved the mystery. Apparently, not all of the aerosol cans recovered from the beach had found their way into the trash. Luckily, we had set the nipa hut as close to the sea as possible before lighting it and thankfully most of the embers fell harmlessly on the wide, sandy beach or in the water. But some did not. We spent a great deal of time and effort scurrying around stomping out little brush fires. After a while though, the danger subsided and we managed to sit around and enjoy what was left of our bonfire. "Enjoy" might not be the best word because we all got yelled at for allowing aerosol cans to end up in the fire. What a public relations disaster that could've been. I could just see the headlines: "American Boy Scouts Bomb and Scorch the Bataan Peninsula."

Jungle Fever

We made the fifty-mile hike to the Bataan Peninsula beach twice. The second time started out much like the first, but with a completely different ending. Sometime during the second day, we came across a little hut just off to the side of the road. I could see water pouring out of one side of it into an adjoining rice paddy. Irrigation water. The sun was unbearably hot, so we took a break and a few of us ran over to take a closer look. Inside was a Filipino lying down taking a nap, his cone-shaped rattan hat resting over his head. The air was cool and refreshing in there. Startled, he sat up quickly, his surprised expression replaced with a wide grin. Apparently his job was to monitor the water flow from the pipe into the adjacent field. He probably had to let it run for a certain amount of time before shutting the valve off. The water was spilling out of the pipe at a tremendous rate as he motioned for us to come further inside the hut. It sure felt good to get out of the sun.

The Filipino could see we were hot and tired. He put his hand in the water and pointed at us and then back at the water, indicating that it was okay for us to do the same. We eagerly ran our hands through the water; it felt cold and looked so clean and clear. Several of the other scouts wetted their faces and dipped their scarves into the water in an attempt to cool down. Before long, we heard the rest of the troop calling for us. They were preparing to resume the hike. The break was over. Those of us in the hut thanked the man for his hospitality as we gathered our things. I was the last to leave and the only one to actually drink some of the water. At the end of the day we had completed forty of our fifty miles. One more night and only ten more miles to go, then we'd be at the beach. Those last ten miles would prove to be the longest and hardest of my life.

During the night, I made several trips to the latrine. Although I was a little tired and my bottom was a little sore, I still felt capable of completing the trip. So the next morning I fell in line and continued the march. After only a few miles, it became clear to me that something was terribly wrong. It was obvious I had a bad case of diarrhea, constantly having to stop and relieve myself. I still felt fine, but every time I drank anything, I had to go. Soon, I was beginning to lag behind as most of the troop marched on ahead to the beach. A small contingent stayed behind to hike with me as pride would not allow me to give up and hop in the truck; not when I was this close to finishing.

Somewhere in that last five miles or so, things began to catch up with me. The hilly terrain, the hot sun, and my apparent dehydration were beginning to take their toll. My bottom became really sore. Each step I took brought pain and before long I was beginning to think I wouldn't make it. I just wanted to stop and give up, but my friends encouraged me to go on. As I became more and more exhausted, I started using a walking stick to help me along. I was thirsty, but drinking water only worsened my condition. I swished water around in my mouth and spit it out to keep myself going.

I don't know how I made it all the way to the beach, but I did. Everybody clapped and cheered. They congratulated me for not giving up. I, of course, felt like an idiot…I should've taken the truck.

The sun was still up when I lay down on the beach beneath the branches of some coconut trees. As the cool winds from the sea blew over me, I drifted off to sleep. Hours later when I awoke, the sun had long since been down and was uncomfortably hot. I was so hot I was sweating and had a tremendous headache. I had a fever.

Saved by a Rabbit Bus

I thought I was going to die on that beach. I couldn't move if I had wanted to, so I figured I might as well die right there. I could hear my friends off in the distance laughing and playing and although somebody would come by occasionally to check on me, I felt so alone. My throat was so sore it hurt every time I swallowed. My head throbbed, my muscles ached, and my bottom was raw. Staring up at the stars, I began to make my peace with God. Actually, it was not quite so dramatic, but what happened next is about as close to a miracle as I've ever experienced in my life. Dad showed up out of nowhere.

Dad! What was he doing here? I just can't express the joy and relief I felt when I saw him. I didn't even know he was coming. He just walked right up and stood over me. He came as soon as he heard I was sick. He hopped a ride on the Rabbit Bus all the way down from Angeles City; Dad always was braver than me.

I felt honored that he dropped everything he was doing and came all the way out there for me. I listened in awe as he described in detail the perilous journey on the Rabbit bus and all the chickens and pigs on board. There was one other thing I'll never forget: he had brought with him a thermos filled with orange juice. Cold orange juice.

Now you must realize the significance of this. For much of the Philippines, and especially the part we were in, neither ice nor refrigeration were readily available. I hadn't had anything cold to drink in over three days and drinking that orange juice was something to remember. It felt so good going down. For the first time that day, everything seemed like it was going to be okay. With Dad there, I felt like such a baby. Not in the bad sense, but in a good sense. I no longer felt alone, I slept better and I even seemed to feel stronger. Even though I was twelve years old, it felt good to sleep with my dad close by. Dad saved me. Again.

The next day, I began to feel better and I could even walk around some, but it literally took several months before I really got back to where I was before I got sick. Over the next few weeks, I lost nearly twenty pounds. The doctors were perplexed at first, but they eventually figured it out. Somehow, I had picked up a serious case of salmonella combined with an even worse case of jungle sprue, a kind of tropical disease that'll rot your gut out. It took a while, but I eventually recovered. I don't know for sure, but I suspect I picked up at least one of those diseases, if not both of them, from the water in that roadside irrigation hut. Dad was right; it's the bug you can't see that'll get you every time.

Years later, my mom and dad told me how worried the doctors were, because at one point, they suspected I might have had cancer. The real sobering thing about all that was where it happened. Thirty years earlier, hundreds of people died along that very same road. How they must have suffered. How anybody survived that death march is beyond me. God bless their souls.

Corregidor

There's an island located several miles south of the Bataan Peninsula and it lies in the 12-mile-wide entrance to Manila Bay.

It's not particularly big and shaped like a giant tadpole, the island is only three and a half miles long. It goes by many names. Some call it the Rock; others the Pearl of Manila. It's more commonly known as Corregidor, the Island Fortress. Fortified first by the Spanish, and then by the Americans, the island had faithfully guarded Manila Bay for years. At one time just prior to World War II, over twenty gun batteries with nearly fifty 12-inch coast artillery guns and 12-inch mortars were in operation on the island. Projectiles for some of the mortars weighed nearly 1,000 pounds. Those mortars could fire a round eight miles in any direction. Yet despite all that firepower, the island fell to the Japanese on May 6, 1942. More than 10,000 American and Filipino defenders surrendered on Corregidor. The American flag wouldn't fly over the island again until March 1945, almost three years later.

I first saw Corregidor from our beach camp the same day after completing my first fifty-miler. I wanted desperately to go to the island. The next day I got my wish.

Bonka Boats

In the morning we all headed down to the shore where several small outrigger boats had been pulled up onto the beaches, presumably our transportation to the island. The boats were just wide enough that passengers had to sit one right behind the other and were only long enough to hold three to four people. At least we didn't have to paddle. All the boats had little motors to propel them across the channel to Corregidor. The natives kept calling them "bonka boats." What a neat name for a boat, I thought. I often wondered what bonka meant, but I never asked.

Soon we were all loaded up and we shoved off into the sea. I was startled to learn how low the boats rode in the water as the water reached right up to the top of the sides. For a minute there, I didn't even think the boats were capable of floating. As soon as we cleared the shore, the operator of the boat reached back and started up the engine. It looked like a lawn mower engine, complete with a hand operated rope crank. Once started, the boat was pointed in the direction of Corregidor Island and off we went. As we chugged along at a leisurely pace, I thought I finally solved the mystery of the bonka boat name. They must have been named after the sounds the engines made, which sounded a lot like "bonka-bonka." At first, the engines would go "bonka-bonka-bonka" and the faster the boats would go, the faster the bonkas went. If I remember correctly, "bonka-bonka-bonka-bonka" was about as fast as they could go.

As we made our way across the channel, I began to feel small. It wasn't long before the shore was far behind us; however, it took a long time before the island appeared to get any closer. It became readily apparent that the island was a lot further away than it looked. I had heard stories of how during the War, Americans swam from Corregidor to Bataan instead of surrendering to the Japanese. The water was surprisingly calm and remarkably clear; yet how anybody could swim that far seemed inconceivable. As the bonka boats sliced through the seawater, the world I was familiar with back on dry land disappeared. Water lapped at the sides and occasionally a small wave would spill over into the boat. I thought we were doomed. Nonchalantly, the driver would scoop out water using a small metal can, like it was no big deal.

One of my friends tapped me on the shoulder and pointed at something just off to the side of our boat. A triangular dorsal fin was keeping pace with us. A chill ran down my back – SHARKS! Oh great. Suddenly the bonka boat I was in seemed even less seaworthy. I was convinced that every little wave we bumped into would be our last. Soon, the shark lost interest and swam away. I saw a few more before we reached the island, but by then the novelty had worn off. Heck, the sharks weren't even very big.

The closer we got to Corregidor the more excited I got and we soon maneuvered into a small harbor. Before long, I was standing on the island. Corregidor was everything I had thought it'd be.

The massive gun batteries, the tunnels, the buildings…even in its present state of ruin, it still looked so formidable. Impregnable. It seemed impossible that anybody could attack the island and live, let alone conquer it. But it did happen – not just once, but twice. The Americans surrendered there in 1942 to the Japanese – and three years later won it back from them.

Corregidor had been pounded with bombs. So many of them, in fact, that there were still entire areas off limits because of all the unexploded ordnance. We were told to carry maps with us wherever we went and to rely on landmarks for orientation, not our compasses. Those, we were told, were useless because there was so much metal on the island.

As we toured around, I found myself wanting to break away from the group and explore. No such luck, though; the scoutmasters watched us like hawks. Since we were only there for a few hours, it was impossible to escape. I had to be content with the tour. I remember the Mile-Long Barracks, the enormous Malinta Tunnels, the disappearing guns of Battery Crockett, Monkey Point and the massive gun at Battery Hearn. I'll never forget that one. The big gun there was mounted by design to face seaward in anticipation of an enemy naval attack. It was so big it couldn't be turned much in azimuth, or side-to-side, only in elevation, or up and down. Since the main Japanese attack came from the Bataan Peninsula, not from the sea, Battery Hearn was almost completely useless. Someday, I vowed, I'd come back and explore the island.

CHAPTER 8

Corregidor Revisited

I made it out to Corregidor two more times before we left the Philippines. The next trip to the island was again by bonka boat, followed by the boring tour, but the third trip – the last time I visited the island – was by far the best; not only in the way I got there, but also because of what I did once I arrived. We arrived on the island by way of an old World War II era Landing Ship Transport, or LST. This time our troop was not there just for the tour, this time we were there for the weekend. I was going to camp there!

The LST we rode on was an active duty ship in the Filipino Navy based out of Subic Bay. The interesting thing about it, though, was the ship was apparently made in Missouri in 1943. I read that bit of information off of a metal plate mounted on a bulkhead just outside the ship's bridge. Sometime after the war, the ship must have been turned over to the Philippine Navy. The LST was a big gray ship, with two big doors in the bow. There was only one cargo hold, just below deck, and it ran the entire length of the ship. The ship's hold was like a huge cave and was designed to carry trucks and tracked vehicles. The doors in the bow could swing open to permit rapid loading and unloading of vehicles, especially on beaches. Today, it was carrying a large contingent of Boy Scouts over to Corregidor. Whoever came up with that idea should've been given a medal.

With all our gear stored below, most of us headed topside to watch the ship leave the port. Subic Bay Naval Facility was a busy port in those days. As we sailed out of the harbor, I imagined we were going off to war. Like my comic book heroes, Sergeant Rock and Sergeant Fury, I felt like I was headed into harm's way. Who knew what adventures lay ahead? I couldn't wait to get to the island.

The Forty Millimeter

The trip from Subic Bay to Corregidor took a little longer than I expected. It didn't take me more than 15 minutes to explore the entire ship, at least the parts I was allowed into. I was already bored. A friend and I had worked our way to the very back part of the ship where we wanted to get a closer look at the 40-millimeter gun mounted back there. As we inched our way up to the gun emplacement, it looked deserted. Carefully climbing up a small ladder, we peered over the edge of the circular retaining wall surrounding it. Just then a head popped up. It was a sailor and before we could think of an excuse for being there, he motioned for us to come on over, so we did. Then he lay back down on the floor, where apparently he had been trying to take a nap before we had disturbed him.

I was in awe in the presence of the gun. Too bad there was no such thing as a Boy Scout artillery merit badge. Before long, I got up enough courage to ask if we could sit on the seats. The sailor, still lying down, motioned that it was okay. There were two seats mounted directly to the gun assembly, one on each side of the carriage. I hopped on one seat, my friend hopped on the other. Both seats had pedals, a targeting site, and a little round wheel with handles. The wheels ran perpendicular to the seats and turning them would rotate the entire gun carriage. The faster you spun the wheels around, the faster the gun would move. One wheel controlled the rotation of the gun, the other controlled the elevation. As the sailor napped, my friend and I rotated and pointed the gun in every direction possible. We imagined we were defending the ship from unrelenting kamikaze attacks. Time passed so quickly that before we knew it the ship had arrived at Corregidor. After raking the rocky coastline with imaginary 40-millimeter rounds, my friend and I left to join the rest of the troop; I didn't want to miss the landing.

We docked at a different part of the island than where we arrived in bonka boats. The boats had landed in an area where the shoreline was extremely rocky and cliff-like whereas the LST docked at a place I'd never seen before. There wasn't much of a beach to speak of; however, there was a large pier. I'm sure I wasn't the only one disappointed that we wouldn't be storming ashore through the LST's big front doors. Just beyond the beach was a small, green-covered flat area that was to be our campsite.

My dad came along on this trip and I'm sure glad that he did. Normally, each patrol would be responsible for bringing enough food for everyone, but this time was different. For some reason each scout had to pack his own food for this trip. Before long, a lot of scouts had exhausted their supply of instant oatmeal, including me. Dad had anticipated this of course and brought extra rations of food along – enough to feed several starving scouts.

Of course, Dad didn't just give the food away, he made us work for it. He mumbled something about the lazy grasshopper and told me to be more like the ant. But, most importantly, bring more food next time. I learned a valuable lesson: plan ahead, bring more food, and always bring Dad along.

We went on another tour again, only this time I paid more attention to the roads. Armed with a map, I was able to form a pretty detailed mental picture of where I was in relation to all of the major gun batteries. I couldn't wait to explore the island.

The Missing Mortar

On my first unsupervised outing, a few other scouts and I headed inland from our camp. The terrain was very rugged and hilly. Although most of the island was covered with vegetation, moving through it was not as big a problem as the jungles on the mainland. The bombing during the war had destroyed much of the original forestation on the island and even after 30 years, the effects were still evident. Soon we came across one of the giant mortar batteries. Earlier on the tour, we learned that this particular battery took a direct hit to one of its ammunition magazines and a horrific explosion toppled many of the mortars. One gun was thrown completely from the battery. According to the tour guide, the piece had never been found. That sounded like a challenge to us. After we finished exploring the battery complex, we set out to find the missing mortar.

The battery was surrounded by large hills, so I knew our search wouldn't be easy. We had no idea in what direction the gun went, or even how far it would have traveled before landing. We split up and began our search.

After a while, I began to suspect there was no gun to be found. Perhaps what really happened was it was damaged so badly in the explosion that it was cut up for scrap or maybe it was blown to bits. I didn't think any of us actually believed we would find the missing mortar, but I thought at least we'd find something. We didn't find anything, not even any bullets. The sun was already down below the hills and soon it would be dark. We had to start heading back.

Just as we began our march down the road, I heard a shout from one of the stragglers. The missing mortar! We quickly scrambled up and over one of the hills and there, about halfway down the opposite side, was the gigantic artillery piece. It was a mortar of the same type from the battery. So it did fly through the air!

Half buried in the hill and partially concealed by the surrounding vegetation, the gun was easy to miss from atop the hill, but we had found it! I was already thinking about the honors and awards that would be bestowed upon us. What a great discovery, perhaps as great as finding a mummy buried in the Sahara Desert. Unfortunately, we were faced with one major problem: the darn thing weighed a ton. Actually, it weighed over 50 tons. Even worse, we found an old Coke bottle in the barrel. Okay, so we weren't the first ones to find the gun, but it was still fun.

The Last Adventure

The next day, my friend and I took off in a new direction. We figured we could cover more ground with just the two of us and we were right. We went down roads and came across places I had never seen. Before long, we were far from the camp. If it hadn't been for the fact that we were on an island, I would say we were hopelessly lost. As we were descending a hill, we came across a rather large piece of concrete. Bunkers and gun emplacements were all over the island and there was nothing unusual with finding structures like this, except the location of this particular one seemed odd. It appeared to be a large, flat slab half buried in the side of the hill. It seemed out of place. Vegetation and even small trees were growing right on top of it, and although there was a road nearby, the slab was well hidden from all directions.

Upon closer inspection, we found this was no ordinary hunk of concrete. It was big – really big. Somehow over the years the slab had become buried in dirt, perhaps on purpose. Walking alongside the edge, I found what appeared to be the top part of a window. Actually, it was more like a rectangular opening. It looked like the slab of concrete we were on was the roof to something. But what?

Tunnels

We dug the window out and peering inside we saw...darkness. But this darkness had an echo to it which meant there was a room in there. I could feel air inside, cool air. I couldn't help but think that we'd found something big. We had brought our flashlights along just for this purpose and we excitedly dug them out of our backpacks. I held my breath as the beams from our flashlights sliced through the shadows. Inside lay a small room and an open doorway on the opposite side. More darkness lay beyond that. There were no bottles, cans or trash. I was really excited now. This room, although empty, appeared to be undisturbed. Wary of booby traps, we threw rocks and sticks inside to see if anything would explode. Satisfied nothing was rigged to kill us, we both squeezed our way through the opening. We thought we had stumbled upon a long-lost bunker, perhaps even a small antechamber to a forgotten tunnel network. The absence of any graffiti meant nobody had been there recently.

However, the uncertainty of what lay beyond the doorway was quickly bringing me closer to a heart attack. I wanted to explore further, but the fact was, I was scared – real scared. For some reason we spoke only in whispers. As our whispers echoed inside the chambers, our imaginations got the better of us. Our own hushed words became the voices of dead ghosts or something stupid like that. Whatever lay in my imagination, it made the hair on my neck stand on end. At one point, we ran over each other scrambling out of there.

Another Plan

Outside we were able to calm ourselves down and together we pieced together a plan. Some plan. We loaded our backpacks with rocks (ammunition) and scrounged up some big sticks (weapons). Climbing back into the underground room, we once again approached the doorway. Shining our flashlights into the dark, we put our plan in motion. We tossed rocks around the corner, no explosions, no screams, no growling or shuffling sounds. We figured it must be safe.

We continued our exploration by tossing rocks in whatever direction we wanted to go. The hallway seemed to have no end, but I think that's because we moved at a snail's pace. We found another room, but it, too, was empty. It had a window like the one before, but this one was boarded up. I could see dirt through the cracks in the boards. Presumably, dirt lay on the other side. We decided to travel down the hallway just a bit more before turning back. We turned our flashlight beams into the next room expecting to find nothing. I was startled to see there was something in there. What I saw was unbelievable.

Unimaginable Treasure

Guns! A lot of guns! There were machine guns, rifles, pistols and even a bazooka! We were stunned. After all my adventures, all my searching and exploring, here at last lay the greatest treasure in all the world. I fought back the urge to leap in there and pick something up. We were still cautiously afraid of booby traps. I heard countless stories about wires attached to grenades, rifles rigged to shoot legs off, and even little crossbow arrows that could put an eye out. After a careful flashlight sweep of the doorway, we entered the room.

There didn't seem to be any rhyme or reason to the placement of the weapons on the floor. Some were stacked against the wall, but most were just lying around, almost as if the weapons had been tossed in there. Another mystery was the wide assortment of weapons. Most of the guns I recognized. There were several different types of rifles, mostly American, but some were definitely Japanese. There were .30 caliber machine guns and even a few Browning Automatic Rifles, or BARs. I had never seen one of those in real life before, but I recognized it from my comic books. By far the biggest weapon in the room was a huge .50 caliber machine gun. So much for booby traps. We could no longer hold back and were soon touching everything. The .50 caliber machine gun was so heavy I could hardly move it. We were like kids in a toy store. Actually, we were more like kids in an armory. I picked up the bazooka. For some reason, I expected it to be much heavier. As it turned out, it seemed lighter than most of the pistols. It was nothing more than a thin-walled tube of metal. I never thought I would find myself saying this, but the bazooka was boring.

It didn't take us very long before we had touched every weapon, but what were we going to do with all of them? For years I had dreamed of finding a room like this and now that I had, I didn't know what to do. It would be difficult to smuggle any of these guns back to the mainland undetected; heck, it would be impossible. If we were lucky, maybe we could sneak a pistol or two back. As hard as it was to leave, we decided we needed to head back to camp. We swore to keep the room a secret just between ourselves and decided not to bring anything back with us, just in case somebody questioned where we got such a thing. As it turned out, that was one of the better decisions we made that day.

The journey back to the campsite was something I'll never

forget. The joy of having found such a treasure was so tremendous that at times, I found myself almost running. I remember reaching camp late in the evening. Small campfires could be seen sprinkled throughout the area, and the smell of food filled the air, but mostly burning oatmeal. It's amazing what we ate while camping. Most of the food we consumed wouldn't normally be given to the dog back home. However, under these circumstances, I'd eat just about anything, even if it fell in the dirt. Today it's called the ten-second-rule. After dropping food on the ground, as long as it's picked up before ten seconds elapsed, then it's okay to eat. But, after having just discovered the find of the century, I would settle for eating dirt. I was more excited than I was hungry – and I guess it showed.

Damage Control

Some of my closer friends knew something was up as soon as we arrived in camp. After several I-swear-I-won't-tell-anybody's, I finally caved in and told someone else. Of course, almost the whole camp knew something was up by bedtime. I was lousy at keeping secrets. We all were, especially secrets like this one.

Word got around that someone had discovered a weapons cache of some sort. That was bad. Once adults got wind of something like that, there was no telling what could happen. Chances were the EOD would be flown in from the mainland. I could just imagine them blowing up the whole place. What a waste.

Fortunately, thirteen-year-old boys were just as bad at repeating gossip as they were at keeping secrets. Sure enough, the whole camp eventually heard about it. The stories ranged from somebody finding the skeleton of a dead Japanese soldier still wearing his uniform, to some poor kid stumbling into a bunker full of poison covered punji sticks and grenade trip wires. Talk about damage control. Almost every version of the rumor I heard had some truth to it, but nothing even came close to reality. And if by some chance it did, I'd make sure I mutated the rumor a bit more before sending it on its way. By the time any adults got around to asking me if I knew anything about any weapons, all I had to do was shrug my shoulders and look dumb. Nobody knew what was going on or if anything had even happened at all. Piece of cake – there was still hope we could salvage something from this mess.

Having learned our lesson from the near disaster of having to share the treasure with everybody, a small band of friends was assembled and sworn to double and triple secrecy. We set out for the bunker at first light in the morning. The trip back was just as exciting as the day before – only this time I had plans to go home with a rifle or something. We were going to try and smuggle stuff back rolled up in the tents. One guy wanted a bazooka really bad. He swore he could buy ammunition for it back in Angeles City. I don't think anybody really believed he could, but nobody argued with him anyway. What if he really could? It would be interesting to see a bazooka blow something up.

Back Inside

It was still very early in the morning when we turned off the road to find the bunker. If I remembered correctly it wasn't far off the road. Only now, my friend and I were having trouble locating the exact location of the stupid place. All of a sudden, everything started to look the same. Part of the problem was we were trying to approach the bunker from a slightly different direction than we had originally discovered it from. That was all it took to get us lost. After spending some time scrambling around trying to locate it, things started to unravel. Time was running out. Soon, everybody back in the camp would be awake and it wouldn't be long before we'd have to go back to the mainland. My friend and I were arguing over which direction we should go next while the rest of the group was beginning to wonder if there really was a bunker. I was beginning to wonder the same thing myself. Walking around in a panic, we finally found it. Suddenly, all the self-doubt was gone; back again was the feeling of pure excitement.

We entered the bunker through the same window as before, only this time the hallways didn't seem as scary. It was unlikely that anybody had set any booby traps from the night before. Nonetheless, some of the new people we had brought along were amazed we were brave enough to squeeze into the window in the first place. I think stupid would have been a better word. Soon, I was back in the main treasure room.

I still had a hard time believing my luck. There were so many weapons, plenty for each one of us to have at least ten or more apiece. With all of us standing there looking at the weapons like that, it didn't take long before all heck broke loose, kind of like what I imagine a shark feeding frenzy would look like after a transport loaded with cattle crashed on a reef. Unfortunately, there was only one bazooka and everybody seemed to want it. Man, it's a good thing nothing was loaded. A few of those arguments over who got what would've ended in bloodshed. Still, we managed to collect our wits enough to realize we couldn't take it all. Besides, a lot of those weapons seemed incredibly big. Before long, everybody had settled on what to take back to camp. If we kept our mouths shut, I figured we could always come back someday, somehow. With that brilliant plan, we headed back to the camp.

Lost Secrets

I don't know if you have ever had the pleasure of watching young people, especially young boys, try to keep a secret, especially one of this magnitude. It must've been hilarious to the casual adult observer. Our downfall came when one of the scouts miscalculated just how hard it would be to hide a Thompson machine gun in his backpack. Boy, were we stupid. We weren't back at the campsite for more than ten minutes when news of the weapons tomb spread. Great, I thought, now everybody knew, including the scoutmasters. Heading back to the discovery site was one of the hardest things I've ever done in my life. Now I would have to share it with everybody. I had this terrible feeling of regret over how this whole situation was turning out.

We led a small contingent of people to the site and soon I was back inside the weapons room for yet a third time. Somehow I hoped something positive could be salvaged from this debacle. Perhaps it was possible there were enough weapons for everyone. That seemed unlikely, though. Even if there were enough weapons for everyone, I had this feeling that none of us would be allowed to keep anything. The room was the way we left it. Still full.

One of the scoutmasters commented on how weird it seemed these weapons were in such remarkably good shape; another pointed out the wide variety. It did appear particularly odd to find so many weapons of different national origins stored in one spot. That was weird. Why would anyone thirty years ago store piles of old American and Japanese weapons in one place…and then forget about them? Just about that time, a light could be seen down one of the dark corridors and it was approaching our position from the opposite direction. Somebody else was in the bunker! Everybody stopped talking and looked down the hall.

The Mysterious Man

Soon a man appeared. He was carrying a flashlight and was wearing a uniform of some sort. The man, obviously a Filipino, started to smile as he approached our position. It seemed he recognized us as part of the Boy Scout contingent that was camping on the island. I just stared at him. We all did. Still grinning, he nodded at us a couple of times as he shined his light in the room with all of the weapons. Then, apparently satisfied that nothing was wrong, he turned around and left. The man went back the way he came. Just like that. Incredulous, we all looked at each other and without so much as a word, we began to follow him. I remember seeing his flashlight beam fade in and out as we followed. Before long, the corridors began to fill with sunlight as we were obviously approaching an opening in the bunker. Soon we reached a chamber that was flooded with daylight from outside. We were in a museum! The mystery man was a museum attendant.

Talk about adding insult to injury. Not only was I not allowed to keep any weapons, but I had to endure slanderous accusations that I was robbing a museum. It appeared that all my friend and I had found was a store room, not some long ago forgotten armaments cache. Apparently, the museum had so many artifacts that not all of them could be displayed at one time. That explained the mumbo jumbo arrangement and assortment of items in one room. All my friend and I really found was a window long ago thought buried in the back of a bunker used as a museum. What a major disappointment. The ride back to the mainland on the LST was not nearly as exciting as the ride out to the island. Still, it was an adventure I'll never forget.

CHAPTER 9

Treasures: Found and Lost

1975 had arrived. There was talk around the house of a new assignment back to the States. My time in the Philippines was coming to an end. I never did find a buried tank but once, while walking with my dad in a ditch, I found a nose cone to a rocket. It was a late World War II vintage of the type usually found on the Chance Vought F4U Corsair that dominated the Pacific skies in the latter part of the war. Japanese pilots had a special name for the F4U, they called it Whistling Death. Next to an old rusted up Japanese rifle, bayonet, helmet and canteen, that rocket nose cone was my most prized possession. Unfortunately, I lost it.

The Home Run

I hit my first and only home run of my life that last year. It was very special for three reasons. One, it was the last game of the season and nobody on our team had ever hit a home run. Heck, in our entire little league, only one other home run had been hit the whole season. Second, it was the game winning hit. Third, and most importantly, I hit that home run right after I bet my older brother Mark a dollar that I'd hit one. Mark was a home run hitter in his league and he constantly teased me about my lack of home runs. It was gratifying to smack that ball out of the park.

Incident at Friendship Gate

Once on my way to school one morning, just as our bus was entering the base at Friendship Gate, I heard a gunshot. As expected, the gate was quickly locked down. The vehicle we were on halted right alongside the checkpoint station. Peering out of the left-hand side of the bus, I could see down onto the gate area. There, alongside the bus, lay a security policeman, a pool of blood around his motionless body. He was apparently dead. Another security policeman calmly checked for a pulse before covering the man on the ground with a blanket.

Friendship Gate was shut down for what seemed like an hour with traffic literally backed up for miles. By the time we were allowed to drive away, the dead man's blood had soaked the blanket. Evidently, the shooting was accidental. A security policeman inside the guard shack was playing with his revolver when it discharged and hit his buddy in the back. In a moment's time, one life was lost forever; the other shattered. Guns are dangerous things.

Wars: Past and Present

I learned a lot about history and human nature. I walked in the shadows of epic battlegrounds and learned of heroic tales. The very names of the places I visited gave me a knowledge I didn't even realize I was learning. Years later, both in high school, college and beyond, that knowledge has served me well. I learned about people like Douglas MacArthur, Gus Grissom, and Billy Mitchell – people who helped shape and define our country. At the time, I had no real clue who these people were or what they did, but I remembered their names. I learned of a war fought long ago and the tremendous impact it still had over thirty years later – and I had a sideline view of a war in progress.

By early 1975, things were going badly for South Vietnam; the North was clearly winning the war and it wouldn't be long before the South would collapse. At the time I didn't know much about that war, like why it started or how long it had been going on, but I did know one was going on. I had friends in school whose fathers fought there; many had fathers who flew missions over Southeast Asia during the day and were home in time for dinner. Some never came home.

The Searchers

One day our troop was on a hike far outside the base's perimeter. We were trekking along dirt roads and as usual it was hot, dusty, and generally unbearable – normal weather when it wasn't rainy, muddy, and even more unbearable. A few miles out, we came across a small group of people resting alongside the road. Several men in the group were heavily armed. Strange looking group, I thought. As we got closer, I could see that the armed men were Filipinos and the unarmed men in the group were Japanese. The Japanese were searching the countryside for their countrymen's remains from the war. They showed us some bones they had recovered. It was a strangely solemn occasion. Everybody spoke in whispers. I'm not sure why, but it seemed like the proper thing to do at the moment.

After we had moved away from the main group, one of the armed men explained that the Japanese had been searching this particular area for many days now and had recovered several skeletons. Also recovered were some artifacts of interest, in particular, samurai swords. The Japanese were also paying cash for information which led to the recovery of any of these items which they cherished so dearly. It seemed like such a strange expedition. On one hand it seemed to be so noble a gesture, the Japanese wanting to bring back home what they so desperately sought. On the other hand, the armed men accompanying the searchers were there to protect the Japanese from being killed. Some hatreds never die.

LINEBACKER

Once, my father stopped the car alongside the road near the flight line. I could see airplanes taxi down the runway, lift off and fly almost directly over my head. I had seen planes from this vantage point before, but this time was different; most of these were bombers...B-52 bombers. The noise was tremendous. The sky was filled with them, many painted jet black. They were on their way to bomb Vietnam. Operation LINEBACKER had begun and it would continue around-the-clock for over ten days. It was eerie watching those planes take off.

Prisoners of War

I had the opportunity to be in the Philippines when the American involvement in Vietnam was ending. I saw American Prisoners of War walk off planes to greet their families; some of those families had been separated for as long as eight years. It was inconceivable for me at 12 years old to imagine just how long eight years was.

When the Prisoners of War visited our classrooms, they talked to us and smiled. I could never figure that one out. Those men had been tortured and held in captivity for years, yet they were able to smile and laugh. I never heard a complaint from any one of them. I never want to go to war.

Babylift

When Saigon fell, our schools closed down to make room for refugees from the mainland to stay; orphans from Operation Babylift were the first to arrive. I remember hearing about the first Babylift flight to leave Saigon; a fully loaded C-5 transport plane crashed and burned with no survivors. Other flights did make it, though. My sisters helped process some of the children through the food lines as the refugees arrived. They told me how some kids crammed hotdogs and other stuff into their pockets because the children weren't used to seeing all of that food. Not knowing when they would eat again, the children took as much as they could. I was glad I didn't have to worry about food.

The Filipino Spirit

One thing I'll never forget was the vividness of the poverty almost everywhere we went. The Philippines is an incredibly poor country. We visited a country club in Manila once and it was beautiful; I even saw part of a polo match. Yet, within that same city, people actually lived in the city dump. Homes were literally carved out of mountains of trash. It was bewildering to me. I just couldn't understand it.

Many of the Filipinos I met exuded a sense of joy and hope about life that's almost indescribable. At times, I was proud to be in their country and at other times, the despair and hostility I felt was almost unbearable. While some people loved me simply because I was from America, others hated me for the very same reason. It was a stinging tutorial I'll never forget.

My Bike

I came home one day to find our house empty. The movers had just left the house. Dad was out sweeping off the driveway and I remember it was still daylight out. Except for him, nobody else was around. I said hello and Dad stopped sweeping long enough to say hello back and rub the top of my head like he always did. My heart skipped a beat when I saw my bike leaning up against the wall in the carport. The movers forgot to pack my bike! This was a catastrophe. I tried to explain to Dad that if we hurried we could catch them before they got too far away – there was no time to waste.

Dad kept sweeping. He didn't appear worried at all. Either that, or he was faking it pretty good. After a rather long pause, he said the movers had to leave some stuff behind because there wasn't enough room for everything.

My level of hysteria began to rise because the only thing I saw left behind was my bike, and Dad – like nothing was wrong – just kept right on sweeping. Just then some kid walked by our house. Dad stopped sweeping and called him over. What was he up to? I thought. Dad asked the kid if he wanted to buy the bike in the garage. The kid took a quick look at it. "Sure. How much?" he asked

"How much you got?" my dad asked. I was stunned…Dad was selling my bike? Before I could say a word, the kid pulled some money out of his pocket and showed it to my dad.

"Is this enough?" the kid said.

"Sure is," my dad replied. "It's all yours."

With a smile about as big as you would expect to find on Christmas morning, the kid hopped on my bike and pedaled away. Dad turned and gave the money to me.

"Here you go, son. This belongs to you."

Still in a state of shock, I reached out as he put the money in my hand and went back to sweeping. I stood there in disbelief at what had just happened – Dad sold my bike for $3.12.

As I watched my bike disappear over the horizon, a weird feeling came over me. I was strangely calm. My dad was still sweeping. The sun was low in the sky. Sad my bike was gone, I no longer felt hysterical. If I didn't know any better, I'd swear I just learned something…something to do with saying good-bye and moving on. Of course, I didn't realize that at the moment. All I could think of was how badly I just got ripped off.

The Amnesty Box and Charlie

The last thing I remember about Clark Air Force Base was the amnesty box just outside the flight line terminal. I walked up and dropped what little remained of my bullet collection. There was not much left, just a few bullets. Most of it I had already traded away or given to my friends.

We even had to leave Charlie, our dog, behind. That was sad. Charlie was born in the Philippines and it was probably his destiny to stay behind. Either that or Dad couldn't afford the fees required to ship him stateside. I always imagined Charlie led an exciting life after we left. Heck, he probably had something to do with the fall of the Marcos Regime.

Travis Air Force Base, California 1975

My family had been away from the States for three years. I arrived in the Philippines when I was eleven years old. I left when I was fourteen. What a shock it was to land at Travis Air Force Base, California and turn on the television. I couldn't believe how much had changed in just three years. I think I spent the next three making up for it. What a waste.

CHAPTER 10

Mount Pinatubo

I haven't made it back to the Philippines since 1975, but I always dream I will someday. Unfortunately, the Clark Air Force Base that I knew is gone. It was destroyed when Mount Pinatubo erupted in 1991. Located just ten miles from Clark Air Force Base, the whole time I was in the Philippines I never even heard of that volcano. Interestingly enough, my younger brother David was at the base during the eruption; he was in the Air Force stationed at Clark at the time.

A large eruption seemed imminent and a decision was made to evacuate the families. David's family was moved to Subic Bay just in time and he was left behind for some reason vital to the National security of the United States (I think he was guarding the mail.) The volcano's eruption coincided with a tropical typhoon rolling through the region. What followed, according to David, was something just short of hell. It became so dark from the falling ash that by midday he was unable to see his hand at arm's length. An eerie orange glow could be seen whenever lightning struck the ground. Sounds were abnormally amplified because of all the ash particles in the air. Thunder crackled through the air with the most unusual reverberations. Dave said he could hear buildings buckling, then collapsing, under the weight of the spewing ash. It was like death had cast a shadow upon the land. The ash and mud were so thick that the flight line had become unusable and too costly to recover. It would take years to clean it up. When it was all over, Clark Air Force Base was officially abandoned by the United States.

The Dictionary

As a Captain in the Air Force, I've had the opportunity to travel quite extensively across the United States. Once, I found myself in Seattle, Washington with some time on my hands. My plane had arrived early in the afternoon and the hotel room I had reserved was not yet ready. With some time to burn, I remembered seeing a library on my way from the airport to the hotel, so instead of sitting around the hotel lobby, I headed back to the library. I figured I had at least enough time to write a letter.

I looked for a nice quiet spot in the library to sit and write and since the reference cubicles are usually the best locations, I sat down at one. There, right before me on a little shelf, was a small dictionary buried in with all of the other reference books. However, this was no ordinary dictionary – it was a Filipino-English dictionary.

I think I must've spent nearly 30 minutes browsing through that book. Tagalog was an amazingly phonetic language. I looked for the words "sari-sari", but all I could find was the word "sarili," which means "self." Maybe those were self-self stores and not sorry-sorry stores after all. I came across the word "banyo" which means "bathroom." Now, that would've come in handy. Perhaps the greatest revelation of all was when I came across the word "bangka." Bangka means boat. Holy cow, I thought, those were Bangka boats, not bonka boats! I felt like an idiot.

I don't regret that I never learned the language while I was in the Philippines…only that I never tried.

Memories

Shortly after I started writing this account about my time in the Philippines, I visited my parents' house in search of any tangible evidence of my adventures. Of course, I still had an old Japanese helmet, canteen, bayonet and rifle. The rifle is nothing more than a rusted shadow of its former self, I can't even see all the way down the barrel.

I found a box with some stuff I saved from the Jungle Survival School. In it was a deck of survival cards, a hand-held flare gun, a small survival booklet that fits in a shirt pocket, some pieces of parachute cord, iodine tablets for purifying water, a few matches dipped in wax to keep the moisture out, a piece of fishing line with a couple of hooks, and various other bits and pieces of junk.

The deck of survival cards is interesting. On one side of each card there is a photographic picture of a jungle plant; on the other are some words explaining how to find the plant and, if necessary, how to cook it. Equally important are the words which explain what to do if you eat something that's not edible.

The small hand-held flare gun is nothing more than a pin gun. Not much bigger than a large Magic Marker, the gun holds a small flare cartridge at the top. It's fired by sliding a spring-loaded pin down and releasing it. As the pin springs up and hits the bottom of the cartridge, the impact ignites the flare and sends it hurtling skyward or in whatever direction the small gun happens to be pointed. All theoretical of course. I've never had the opportunity to fire the hand-held flare gun. I'm guessing it'd probably be a good idea to wear heavy gloves.

I still had a lot of my old Boy Scout stuff. I had most of my merit badges, including the M-16 Rifling Merit Badge, and most of the patches I'd earned or otherwise collected while in the Philippines – including my treasured 50 Miler patches and the accompanying Bataan Death March medals. The 50 Miler patch is the standard Boy Scout patch awarded to any scout who has completed a 50-mile hike, but the commemorative medals are really unique. I earned one for each time I completed the march.

Each medal has a small engraved illustration on the front and depicts three men helping each other as they struggled on the Bataan Death March.

I found a lot of photographs; none of them are in mint condition, at least by professional standards. Almost all of the pictures are out of focus or have faded, but they're priceless to me. My favorite one is of my little brother David and I as we're standing next to a huge artillery piece located on Corregidor. The cannon is pointing seaward, away from the Manila Bay. If I'm not mistaken, that's the Battery Hearn site, the infamous wrong-way cannon. There are several pictures of various campsites, hikes and swimming meets; there's even a picture of the big python snake we captured in our backyard. And last, but not least, there's a picture of my dad struggling to maintain his composure during the roadside ant attack.

Old Letters

Amidst all that lost treasure I found several old letters. They were written to me by a few of the closest friends I ever had in the Philippines. The letters are some of my most valuable possessions. Shortly after leaving, I received a letter from Bill, who was still in the Philippines when he wrote it. Bill and I had many adventures together. Here are a few excerpts, mistakes included:

Dear John,

How are things going? Just after you left the troop went to Camp O'Donnell, Dave made a deal with 363 that we would have a swim race with them, and the losing scoutmaster had to wash the others dishes. Naturally we won. The troop just got back from Subic. We went down to Boton and spent the night, then that morning we left to go 5 miles into the jungle but got lost and ended up going 10 miles. We camped by a river in a nice spot, and after lunch we all went down the river in a nice spot about 2 miles in our underwear, because nobody had a bathing suit. The next day we found a shortcut and we hiked 5 miles back. Dave was driving the bus back and hit a mud hole and mud went all over the windshield. So we all had a nice time

cleaning it off. The patrols in the troop are now Pirate, 1st Aussie DIVISION, and the great BUNNY PATROL. After you left the whole patrol (eccept me) wanted to change the name. Mr. Anderson is going to be our new scoutmaster when Dave leaves. Bataan is going to be fun next year. It will last 7 days and we will spend 3 days in Corregidor. The only thing to me that will be bad, is that we have to go the whole 50 miles for the medal. I got a helment that is in perfect condition except for the rust. I have the first aid kit you left, know other patrol has a good one because we get our supplies from them. HA, HA. Where are the rubber gloves that were in the first aid kit? When we got back from Subic, Daves car had a flat because someone put a nail in it. Dave got the new ponchos and canteens in and the ponchos don't have any holes to make a tent like he said, and the canteens are so thin you can poke a hole in them. While we were at the leader ship campout me, Durr and Don skipped most of the classes and went and had dirt clod wars. Don was backing up and fell in one of the ditches. Then about five minutes later we quit, we were walking back and he fell back in because he didn't have his glasses on. When we went to Camp O'Donnell me and Rank hit Anderson in the mouth the same time I hit Gary in the mouth, so we were happy. Got to go now. I sure wish you were still here with your motorcycle so we could get caught again.
YOUR FRIEND
BILL

Good old Bill. It was nice to read that letter again after all those years, but I have no idea what happened to the rubber gloves. Or Bill. I received a few more letters from him over the years but nothing more after that. I suspect he may have joined the Air Force when he got older, just like me. I wonder if Bill has any of my old letters. It'd be interesting to see if I spelled that bad as a fourteen-year-old. I'll save the motorcycle story for another book.

Another good friend of mine was Tom. At one time, he and I were inseparable as friends, but as so often happens with childhood friends, we drifted apart. Still, for a time anyway, Tom was my best friend and I still miss him occasionally. He left the Philippines before I did and moved to Florida with his family. I wrote him a letter and he responded with one of his own. Here are a few words from that letter:

Dear John

I am fine, it was a surprise getting your letter. But I'm glad I did. I'm writing this letter the same day I received yours, and today I brought that picture of the python we caught in your backyard to school. It brought a lot of good memories.

I'm into skate boarding, along with everybody else. I play soccer now on a brand new team here. and I'm going to get some puma's. I take gymnastics. And I'm still in scouts.

I wish we were together again. We made a good team.
Your Friend,
Tom. Age 14

Another friend was Mark, not to be confused with Mark my older brother, this Mark was my age. If there was one thing I liked about Mark, it had to be his letters; he wrote me often. Here are some of his words:

Dec. 8, 1975

John,

I just got your letter 5 min ago.

We started fixing up are New Scout Hut, it's across from our old hut.

I'm second class now and of course Bill still is!

Durr moved to Florida somewhere around Tom.

Don is a life scout still, he joined football and was on the eagles he was pretty good. He had to quite because he faild a class.

Mr. Anderson is going to be our new Scoutmaster in two months.

Dave is living in late March.
Do you have Tom's home address?
A kid named Mitchel moved into your house.
He's pretty cool.
I have to do my *@#?) homework now

Merry Christmas
Your Friend
And
Dear Buddy
And
Death Marcher
Companion
Mark

Judging from his penmanship and grammar, Mark needed to do that homework. Along with his words came a couple of cartoons drawn on the back of the envelope, one shows a rather two-dimensional person standing with his legs bent at the knees, like the person is squatting. The cartoon person is saying, "I can't make it." And next to that are the words "<u>Do You Remember</u>?" complete with the underline. An obvious reference to me trying to hike the last ten miles of our fifty-miler into Mariveles on the Bataan Peninsula. I received another letter from Mark just a few months after his first one.

John,
    How are you doing? Im doing fine.
    I have some news that you wont believe! So set down before I tell you. Are you ready? Bill, made First Class! (After you finish fanting reed the rest of my leater)
    Where moving soon, to Washington D.C.; Dave is moving to the same place. My dad is going to go to the war collage.
    Where going to the Capones in one week; its going to be for four days.
    Where are going to be alwode to go snorkeling and fising. For any new scouts where going to bloddy up the water then throw them in for initiation. Cool, uh.
    Almost every one in the troop is second class.
    Kevin is a losyer S.P.L than you ever where.
    Now you know how bad he is. We cant wait to kick him out of this job.
    Im First class now, and I have all my recwierments for

Star done except for the time.

There are two new kids, Jay and Jack there preaty cool.

There hasn't been any exipment to top the time you nut tried to explode that bomb.

John P. quite the troop some time ago, but someone said he might come back.

Im going to take scuba leasons soon, for the final dive they throw you in a pool of sharks with aroast aroulnd your neck and throw you over the of the boat, out in the middle of the ocean.

I cant waite to take the course, it will be ablast!!!!!!!!!!

Ive got to do my homework now, its weird to think that while Im writing you, you are sleeping.

ILL WRITE BACK AFTER WE GET BACK FROM THE CAPONES!

Youre Friend,

Mark

Unlike Mark's first letter, his second letter was typed. Still, I'm not sure how much of his cryptic use of the English language can be attributed to unfamiliarity with the typewriter. I was glad to see he was hanging in there with his homework. As with the other letter, this one had some cartoons as well. One insinuates I set somebody's cot on fire. Man, I sure don't remember that one. The other one refers to an incident involving guard duty. Whenever our troop camped outside the base, it was a matter of policy to post guards to prevent late night robberies by any bad guys lurking about. Well, according to Mark's cartoon, somebody set the guard duty alarm clock ahead by one hour. That somebody then woke up the next person in line to stand guard duty. Nobody figured out until the morning that the clock had been set ahead. By that time, it was impossible to tell who had perpetrated the crime. Pretty clever, if I say so myself.

I'm thankful I had the opportunity to live in the Philippines from 1972 to 1975. I know at times it may have seemed I was unsupervised or unguided in my adventures, yet I truly believe

God was watching over me. I never did find any skeletons. Nonetheless, I did leave the Philippines with something immeasurable, it only took me twenty years to realize it. It's something worth more than any tangible treasure I could've ever laid my hands on – it's called adventure. Pure and simple. It's possible my imagination has gotten the best of me these past twenty years, but that's beside the point. I was lucky to have seen and done things that most people can only read about in a book…and I lived to tell about it.

Only now, with children of my own, do I realize the nightmares my adventures must have given my parents. I write this book as a legacy to my children. Heaven help me if they read it before reaching adulthood, I'll have a lot of explaining to do. And finally, but always, God bless my mom and dad.

The End

ONE LAST THING

There's one last story I wanted to include in this book, but I wasn't sure where to put it, so it ended up here at the end. It happened during my college days, several years after I left the Philippines, in Texas of all places. There's a Philippine connection of sorts, but more importantly, it's a great story worth telling.

The Philippine Frog Monster

During summer break from college, a friend of mine and I worked as swimming instructors for children at a swimming pool in San Antonio, Texas. My friend's name was Doug. Officially we were called counselors because we were hired on as part of the staff for a youth summer camp program at Lackland Air Force Base. Unlike most of the other counselors, Doug and I had it pretty easy. All we had to do was hang out at the pool and basically play with kids all day. There must've been more than 150 kids in the program, but Doug and I never had to watch them all at once. They would show up at the pool in groups, escorted by one of the other counselors. When one group was finished, the next group arrived. The work was easy and occasionally very satisfying, especially when we succeeded in actually teaching someone how to swim.

The rest of the counselors were each assigned a group of kids and spent most of the day with them. They escorted them back and forth from art class to craft class, to lunch, to the pool, and anywhere else the children needed to go. Occasionally Doug and I would make it over to the youth center building just in time for the younger kid's nap time. Sometimes we'd grab a mat and take a nap ourselves – writing that off as nap time supervision. Other times we'd poke our heads in and tell the kids to scream as loud as they could on the count of three. Although Doug and I were popular with the children, I suspect some of the other counselors thought we were pretty shiftless and lazy. Of course, you're probably wondering what this has to do with the Philippines. Well, let me explain...

It all began when the camp director thought it'd be a great idea if the counselors put on a talent show for the kids. All the counselors were to participate, including the two lifeguards. A date was set for the big event and several planning meetings were scheduled so everyone could coordinate their talent show act with the camp director and the talent show committee. Doug and I were convinced the talent show was doomed to fail. None of us had any talent to speak of, so when the time came for the first meeting, Doug and I didn't go. We vacuumed the pool instead. We were positive that, given a little time, everybody would come to their senses and just forget about the whole affair. Unfortunately, everyone else attended the meeting, presented their ideas and the camp director approved them. Then she came looking for us. Thinking quickly, we told the camp director our act was so good that we wanted it to remain a secret, even from her and the rest of the counselors. Given our past reputation, I'm surprised she bought off on that. Of course, Doug and I had no idea what we were going to do. Seeing as how we still had several weeks to go, we didn't worry about it too much; after all, we were college students. Besides, there was still a possibility the whole thing would just fade away.

Time passed and talent show meetings came and went but Doug and I never attended any of them. Instead of fading away, though, the talent show became a highly anticipated event with the kids. What's worse, the most anticipated act of the whole thing was the secret talent show act. Our plan wasn't working at all. The day before the talent show, panic set in. Doug gave me a worried look and asked what we were going to do. We hadn't even discussed any ideas, let alone rehearsed anything. The much anticipated event was tomorrow and everybody was expecting something big from both of us. Even worse, we were scheduled as the grand finale. We were doomed.

I pointed out to Doug that we were only dealing with children here. I mean, we could probably just get up there and wrestle with each other and the kids would love it (now, I wonder where that idea came from.) I told Doug I had a lot of stuff at home we could use as costumes. If we both came in early tomorrow we'd have enough time to think of something.

The next morning, I showed up with a couple of brown paper bags full of stuff I picked up from around the house. I brought in a pair of cowboy boots, a bullwhip, some pantyhose, an Indiana Jones hat, an old WWII German Luftwaffe service jacket and gas mask, a dark green F-4 Phantom drag parachute, and a bunch of other odds and ends. Don't ask me how all that stuff ended up in my house in the first place – that's another story altogether. Doug took one look at the items and asked me if I had any good ideas yet. Okay, now I really started to panic.

Doug and I were still telling everyone our talent show act was a secret, but by the time the show started, I think some of the other counselors were on to us. I think the pantyhose were a dead giveaway. I felt a little better after watching the first act, it was lousy. We were confident we could do better without even practicing. Of course, we had no other alternative.

I'm not sure exactly how I came up with the idea, but somehow the concept for the Philippine Frog Monster was born. Doug liked the name a lot. Unfortunately, we were still working on the details of what a Philippine Frog Monster was when the camp director came up and asked us if we could possibly do two acts. It turned out the talent show acts were running shorter than planned. I guess Doug and I were so excited that we finally had a name for our secret act that we readily agreed to do a second one. Only after she said they needed the second act right now did we realize our folly.

Quickly, Doug rounded up a few of the older kids and told them to do as he said. Doug then donned the Indiana Jones hat and jumped out on the stage and started to tell the story about a big ugly guy with a whip who chased mice. I didn't realize it until then, but Doug was a little weird; nonetheless, he was a good storyteller. He had his assistants squeak around the stage like mice as he told his tale. After a few minutes I popped a cassette tape into the center's stereo sound system. Seconds later, a dance song popular with the children could be heard throughout the building as I stepped out onto the stage wearing cowboy boots, blue jeans, the German Luftwaffe jacket and the pantyhose over my head. With the bull whip in one hand I started to dance around the stage after the mice. The kids playing the mice reacted right on cue and danced around like I was chasing them. The audience went wild as they clapped to the music. Soon the song ended and our act was over. It couldn't have lasted more than five minutes from beginning to end, yet Doug and I got a standing ovation. It was the first one so far. The camp director was so impressed, she told us she couldn't wait to see our secret act…she apparently was still under the impression that we had one. However, seeing as how everybody was so impressed with our last act, Doug and I were pretty confident that whatever the Philippine Frog Monster did was going to be a success. I mean, who would've ever thought a dancing German with a bullwhip, cowboy boots and pantyhose on his head who chased mice would've received a standing ovation? Go figure.

Soon it was time for the grand finale. The curtains were drawn and Doug and I prepared the stage for the Philippine Frog Monster. Since we didn't want to mess with our earlier successful formula, Doug retained his position as narrator and I retained mine as the monster. Doug liked the Indiana Jones hat so much he decided to wear it again. I put the German gas mask on and draped myself with the F-4 drag parachute. Both the gas mask and chute were green. With the stage curtain closed, I crouched down on the floor in a corner along the back of the stage. Doug said I was perfectly camouflaged. As long as I didn't move, nobody would think anything was there except for a pile of green blankets or something. Doug enlisted the aid of a couple of the older kids again to use as natives, but he still wasn't sure what we were doing. After I assured him that I didn't either, he gave the signal to raise the curtain.

Doug began the story of the Philippine Frog Monster by banging slowly on a drum he held in his hands. He told a tale about a horrible monster that terrorized the jungles of the Philippines which the natives called the Philippine Frog Monster. I could hear some hushed oohs and aahs from the audience. At least we were off to a great start. Doug continued…nobody had ever seen the monster and lived to tell about it, but they knew it was there. Somewhere. As Doug spoke he would bang the drum just a tiny bit faster. On cue, the natives would traverse the stage, apparently frightened of the Philippine Frog Monster lurking somewhere in the jungle around them. Doug would bang the drum a little faster and then stop abruptly as one of the kids let out a scream just off stage. After a brief pause for effect, he'd start banging slowly again on the drum. The natives would begin to traverse the stage again, only this time there was one less native than before. This continued on for some time until it became obvious to me that Doug didn't have any idea how to end the story. The uneasy glances he threw in my general direction were definite clues; the fact that he had run out of natives was another. It was time to act.

Slowly I started to raise myself up off the floor. As I did so I began to exhale forcefully out of the gas mask. It was designed such that exhaling in that manner would force the air to vibrate a small rubber exhaust manifold on the front of the mask. The noise it created was very loud and unusual to anyone who hadn't heard it before. Doug banged on the drum faster as I continued to rise and move slowly across the stage towards the audience. This continued right up until I reached the edge of the stage, at which point Doug stopped banging on the drum. The room was strangely quiet. I looked out at the audience to see their reaction. It was a lot like the reaction of the Filipino Boy Scout troop back in the Philippines – everybody just appeared to be sitting there waiting for the punch line or something. Doug and I exchanged a quick glance. We didn't say a word to each other, but we both knew that unless we did something soon we probably wouldn't be getting a standing ovation this time. Seconds seemed to go by like hours. I could feel my forehead beginning to sweat inside the gas mask, but then again, at least I had a mask on. Doug was just standing there with a drum in his hands. After looking over at Doug one last time, I did something which to this day is still a mystery to me. I let out a big yell and jumped off the stage.

I'm not sure what I was trying to accomplish by doing that, but I did manage to land safely just in front of the first row of children. The audience was arranged so the youngest kids sat in front and the oldest in the back. What happened next can best be described as what happens when a large rock is thrown into a perfectly smooth lake. Before I even hit the ground the front row was already beginning to move away from me, or rather, the Philippine Frog Monster. The audience's blank stares weren't because they thought Doug's story or my costume was stupid. Instead, almost every kid in that auditorium thought the Philippine Frog Monster was alive and real. Not only that, but it just jumped off the stage. The children were scared to death.

The screaming began immediately and didn't stop for some time. As soon as the other counselors realized what was happening it was already too late to stop it. The front row ran over the second row on their way to the nearest exit. Any survivors in the second row ran over the third, and so on. The children were stampeding over each other to get out of there as fast as they could. The exits were quickly clogged as kids tried to shove their way to freedom. Traffic outside the youth center came to a halt as screaming children came running out of the auditorium and right into the road.

One of the older boys shouted out that I was the Philippine Frog Monster. None of the younger kids would even stop running or screaming long enough to listen, but a few of the older kids did. Before long I was buried under a mountain of boys as they dog piled on me. I guess that was their way of trying to show the younger kids that the monster could be stopped. Doug said the dog pile was nearly as tall as he was and that the camp director thought I must surely be hurt. I wasn't injured but it did take me a little while before I got a fresh breath of air again. That darn gas mask was hard to breathe in, buried beneath all those kids.

It took a very, very long time to get things calmed down. Some kids weren't convinced the Frog Monster wasn't real until I came back out on the stage and removed the gas mask and parachute in front of them. Even then, a lot of kids went home with little tear streaks on their faces. After all that, Doug and I still managed to win first and second place for the talent show. I think the other counselors didn't do so well because they planned too much. I'm not sure if the camp director got in any trouble with the parents over that incident or not. All I remember was being told there'd be no more secret talent show acts.

As for Doug...well now he's my brother-in-law. Poor guy married one of my sisters.

A NOTE FROM THE AUTHOR

This book was originally written in long-hand between 1994-1995 and was meant only to be read to my children. Through a series of almost comical circumstances it was first published in 1998 through the encouragement of a good friend of mine, Victor Figueroa. Assigned together in the military during the mid-1990's, we spent a lot of time on multiple deployments and assignments. As one might imagine, we became good friends. Victor saw value in this story beyond that of a father writing a bunch of stories for his sons…and how right he was. It was Victor who convinced me to publish, and for that I owe him a debt of gratitude.

Even though the first edition of this book was never widely distributed, the feedback I received from those who did read it was remarkable. Many of my peers have told me the stories in this book remind them of their own often misguided childhood adventures; others, emphatically, that this is a story about Scouting and the pure joy of "just getting out there and doing something." Most surprising have been the comments from moms – mostly the mothers of sons who've told me this story opens a window into their young one's minds like no other; the sheer stupidity and mischief of a boy unfettered by fear to just go out and explore. The one remark I've received more than any other though, was when was I going to write another one.

Years ago my youngest son – after having these stories read to him "just one more time" – wistfully announced just how neat it would be if he and his brothers could go back in time and be with me on these adventures. The concept behind *Running Across the Moon* was born. If you enjoyed reading this book, then that one is a must read.

Nine Thousand Miles to Adventure is nothing more than a call to action to get out and explore one's surroundings, have fun, and to someday reminisce about it all. And of course, to make the stories better as time goes by. This second edition of *NTMTA* was published in an attempt to correct all of the boyish "12-year-old" grammatical mistakes riddled throughout the first. I was worried that in doing so, many of the qualities that made the first edition endearing to so many would be lost. However, I shouldn't have worried – I've been told this edition still reads like a 12-year-old wrote it. And in a way, I'll take that as one of the greatest compliments I've ever received.

John P. Santacroce – 2018

What people have said about the book...

"Entertaining from cover to cover…I lost count of the times I actually laughed out loud."

"A page-turner for young readers as they share John's adventures growing up in the Philippines. Read this unique book and talk about it with your children!"

"Loaded with an adventurous boy's observations and discoveries. I guarantee this book will be a treasured addition to your library, and one that readers of all ages will enjoy!"

"John's first book is an example of a brilliant mind who's put his youthful memories to paper…with amazing results. You'll feel the excitement of a young man as he explores the Philippines."

"I wish my childhood had been this exciting!"

www.ingramcontent.com/pod-product-compliance
Lightning Source LLC
LaVergne TN
LVHW041623070426
835507LV00008B/428